CASTE

by the same author

IMAGES OF INDIA
(Photographs, with an introduction
by Dervla Murphy)

CASTE
At Home in Hindu India

Sophie Baker

JONATHAN CAPE
LONDON

To the memory of my sister,
Charlotte Wolfers

First published 1990
© Sophie Baker 1990

Jonathan Cape Ltd, 20 Vauxhall Bridge Road, London SW1V 2SA

A CIP catalogue record for this book
is available from the British Library

ISBN 0-224-02459-0

Typeset by Selectmove Ltd, London
Printed in Great Britain by Butler & Tanner Ltd,
Frome and London

Contents

Illustrations

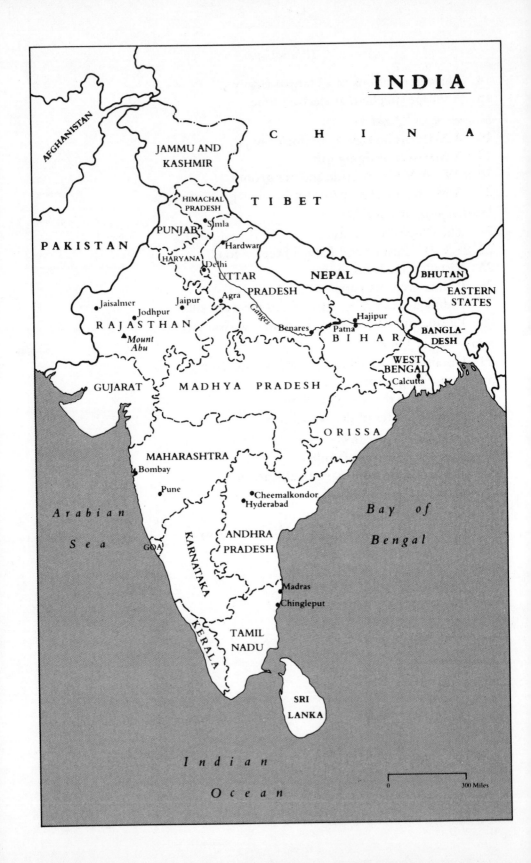

1
First Encounters

In the summer before the Russian army invaded, I was working as a stills photographer with a film unit in Afghanistan. Despite the awe-inspiring landscapes, roamed by exotic nomadic tribes, there was much I did not like about the country. The heat in June was unbearable – it was too hot to walk in the streets after ten o'clock in the morning. I was appalled by the way women seemed to be regarded, many of them completely shrouded from head to foot in that inhospitable climate in a thick drab-coloured cotton burka, their dark eyes peering out from behind a woven grill. In the social hierarchy the family herd of goats seemed to enjoy a more privileged status.

When I was not working I travelled a good deal but failed to penetrate the social mask of Islam. I went up to the northern-most town, Mazar-i-Sharif, stopping on the way to eat charcoal-grilled shashlik of tender lamb morsels dipped in fresh lemon juice. Our driver left us for two hours parked by the unshaded highway while he visited a brothel set up in a tented encampment 50 yards from the road! The bus journey through the glorious Hindu Kush was enchanting, though I did not enjoy the company of the emaciated and stoned Western hippies who talked only of their rotten guts and eking out their dollars to continue their leech-like existence. I resented the assumption that because I was fair-skinned I was a part of their group.

The Afghans are a handsome race, dark haired, with high cheekbones and attractive pale brown skin. The men wear turbans and long jackets in many colours woven in a beautiful tie-dyed design. Before marriage, outside the city, the young girls roam barefoot in the fields, wearing floral-pattern dresses which are adorned with brass trinkets, their large eyes enhanced with black lines of kohl. They disliked being photographed and at the sight of a camera they cursed loudly and often pelted me with small stones.

At the end of my assignment I was ready and eager to return to England. Despite the many invitations from a childhood friend who had been posted to the British High Commission in Delhi, I thrust aside the tempting proximity of India. I had no desire for more heat, still less for the poverty, the mosquitoes and the disease my mind conjured up. Yet I wanted to see my old friend again, and wondered if here was an opportunity I should not let pass. The flight from Kabul to Delhi took little over the hour, the timetable said. In the end I succumbed and postponed my return home.

The journey was to take me across Pakistan, flying over the treacherous Khyber Pass. To give me Dutch courage – for I have never liked air travel – I purchased a litre of over-priced black market white wine from a tourist hotel and passed the journey in an inebriated daze. We touched down at New Delhi airport just as the effects of the alcohol were beginning to wear off.

Stifled by the weeks spent in an atmosphere of rigid Islamic dogma, I was at once overwhelmed by the change in culture. The summer monsoon rains had started, and as I waited patiently to pass through immigration the steamy heat and a heady aroma of betelnut wafted through the hall. I was surprised by the sight of the women in brilliant-coloured chiffon saris, their arms and midriffs bare, and with garlands of marigolds and sweet-smelling jasmin hanging in their hair. I clambered into the back of a scooter-rickshaw, a small carriage attached to the back of a motorbike with three wheels, and held on for dear life as the Sikh driver deftly and speedily manoeuvred the vehicle through a maze of battered black Ambassador cars (modelled on the thirty-year-old Morris Oxford), herds of goats and enormous wooden carts pulled along by large white oxen.

My friend had the good fortune to be staying in a spacious first-floor flat, part of a gracious house which stood back from a large tree-lined avenue in the most luxurious residential area in the city. The house was surrounded by flower beds filled with glorious tropical blooms and immaculately mown and well-watered lawns. Parakeets and other exotic birds perched in the bushes, their chatter and song sounding clear in the still of the falling light. At the gate my bags were taken from me by a charming gentleman in a white turban with a gold-coloured crest.

'Sahib will be home shortly. While Memsahib takes a bath, is there anything to be pressed? Dinner will be taken out.'

I would as soon have climbed into bed, but courtesy and a sense of anticipation helped me overcome my fatigue. On this first night in India I was going to have dinner at the British High Commission and to watch a performance of Gilbert and Sullivan's *H.M.S. Pinafore* by their amateur dramatics society. During the second act I fell fast asleep in my seat.

The next few days were passed in what seemed to me an unreal world. From a position of privilege and comfort I saw something of what I perceived to be a country unlike any other in the democratic world. I went to Agra in an air-conditioned bus to see the Taj Mahal and flew to the holy city of Benares on the Ganges where devout Hindus take the dying so that their remains can be burnt on the banks before the embers are bestowed into the sacred waters. On the steps leading down to the water's edge, emaciated beggars lay in rows, confident that to die here would be to ensure a nobler life the next time round. I wandered through the crowded alleyways of Old Delhi, entranced by the many craftsmen, shopkeepers and vendors of freshly prepared spicy kebabs and special sweets. When I left, I carried a large basket full of fresh mangoes on to the aeroplane, determined to return to see more before the year was out.

Six months later, the coastal region of south-east India experienced one of the worst cyclones and tidal waves ever known. Winds of over 120 miles an hour destroyed thousands of homes and brought ruin and devastation to crops and cattle. An estimated 30,000 people lost their lives and a further 200,000 were left homeless. An international appeal was launched for rehabilitation and more than one overseas

aid agency approached me about the possibility of having their relief work documented – I agreed to go and photograph the misery
suffered. I was impressed by the speed with which the Indians
themselves organised their own rehousing, how they managed to
return to their damaged land and how, within a few weeks, they
prepared optimistically to celebrate the annual harvest festival.

Before long I found myself captivated by some intangible quality
that lay hidden in the soul of this chaotic nation. I was puzzled
and could not understand what it was that kept luring me back,
in spite of the squalor to be found everywhere. Yet in this culture,
so different from that of the West, I felt free and safe to wander any-
where I wished. My presence here excited a curiosity that emanated
warmth and friendliness rather than the hostility I had encountered
in Afghanistan, and each visit served only to intensify the paradox,
instilling in me a desire to keep in touch.

For four years I returned every winter, my trips culminating in a
commission by Christian Aid to take the photographs for an educational slide show which focused on one village in the centre of
India and was designed to illustrate how the caste system operated
in the countryside. I was fascinated by this strange juxtaposition in
people's lives. On the one hand dignity and order were maintained
through technical skills handed down from generation to generation,
yet for many progress was hampered by individual circumstance
of birth. However hard the striving, the situation would remain
unaltered during this lifetime. How had such a state of affairs taken
so firm a grip on the Indian mind, overruling all political measures
taken to improve the people's lot?

The Indian subcontinent is enormous – 2,000 miles wide and
nearly 1,900 miles from north to south, with a coastline of almost
4,000 miles. This massive landmass consists of vast sand deserts,
the most splendid mountain ranges in the world, dense rainforests
and, for the most part, wide and seemingly endless plateaus and
plains. In all, fifteen official languages are spoken and written,
including Hindi, Tamil, Telegu, Urdu, Punjabi and Bengali, and
a further 844 spoken dialects are in everyday use. English is still
the official language of central government. Today the population is
approaching 800 million, and this number is increasing by 20 million

every year. An estimated 70 per cent of that population live in the country's 575,000 villages where life depends almost exclusively on an agricultural economy. City-dwellers are fast approaching an existence as sophisticated as that of the developed West as modern technology takes hold, yet they ride on the back of a society that remains almost mediaeval. By the time I had completed my mission it was clear to me that nothing could be understood about Indian life unless one understood the subtleties of the caste system that permeated every corner of it.

When I next returned to India it was after an absence of five years and much had altered in the cities. Video recorders and modern Japanese cars were now commonplace, yet in the village where I had worked, apart from the children I had known growing up, the introduction of electricity and two diesel-engine-operated water pumps were the only change.

I was determined to get beneath the surface. To my great relief, persuading families to discuss their lives with me was not at all difficult. The main hurdle was communication, and finding interpreters who were both sympathetic and efficient proved more of a problem. I persevered, acknowledging that there would be inevitable gaps or important information withheld.

I began by mixing business with pleasure and visiting one of my favourite areas in India, the desert state of Rajasthan, setting out from Delhi with some Indian friends and my small son. I had previously arranged to meet a young woman who claimed that her royal ancestors came from the bordering state and that she spoke the local dialect. I was soon to discover how so many Indians have the delightful but infuriating habit of trying to please you by distorting facts and saying what they think you want to hear rather than telling the truth. This can be attributed to their dislike of saying 'no', hence promises are made which they are unable to fulfil. My Indian princess certainly had royal connections but her command of the language was even less fluent than my evening-class Spanish.

Jaisalmer in Rajasthan is nearly 200 miles due west of Jodhpur, the former home of many a deposed maharaja. Rising magnificently out of the Thar desert is the handsome fifteenth-century sandstone fortress in and around which the city is built. In the last hundred years many Brahmin communities (families of hereditary priests) who formerly farmed the land and upheld the state economy have left their arid estates and migrated inland towards more fertile country, and now countless ruined cenotaphs lie abandoned at the base of the fortress walls. It is the staunch Rajputs, previously warriors and protectors of the Kshatrya caste (a social division that will be explained in the third chapter) who have doggedly remained, attempting to raise their cattle in the surrounding desert. Despite the hardship imposed by a cruel and unyielding climate, it is an area where dacoity (organised crime) is unknown and where people on the whole live peaceful and harmonious lives.

We travelled there on the overnight train which leaves Jodhpur every evening at ten o'clock and heads towards the border of Pakistan. It delivers the mail, fresh fruit and vegetables and other consumable goods on the way, stopping several times before reaching its final destination at seven o'clock the following morning. Despite the heat, we were recommended to keep our compartment windows tightly closed to prevent us being coated with a thick layer of fine yellow sand. On arrival our party settled into one of the more comfortable hotels and with the help of the hotel manager I set about meeting a family who would be willing to talk to me.

2
A Princely Family
of Rajputs
in Rajasthan

That evening my interpreter, the princess, and I went by jeep to meet Bhawar Singh, the head of a cattle-farming Rajput family, who lived on his estate some 20 miles from Jaisalmer. While the princess disappeared into the farm house to talk to the women folk, I walked round taking photographs and handing out polaroid snaps to the children who kept following me. At first I was apprehensive. I did not wish to appear too intrusive, preferring to let everyone become accustomed in their own time to having a European look inside their home and ask personal questions. I was confused, too, by all the people who had come to stare. Visitors were rare and a reason for everyone to stop what they were doing and gape. I realised that for this family to accept me I would have to spend long periods with them until I was no longer an object of curiosity.

Before leaving, I was approached by Bhawar Singh's wife who invited me into the home to drink tea. Both she and her daughter-in-law had their faces covered but I was assured that when they came to know me better they would relax and lift their veils. As I left, the daughter-in-law handed me a piece of paper on which was written the name and regiment of a distant uncle living in Delhi. I was implored to discover his whereabouts.

On the way back to the hotel I asked my interpreter what she had discovered. Little had been disclosed, it seemed, although the younger woman was in some distress and had pleaded to be taken away. If I could contact these relatives of hers, maybe something could be done.

Before my next visit I sent the family a batch of enlarged photographs and sought out the man whose name I had been given. At the headquarters of the Raj Rifles in Delhi three men answered to this name. I wrote them all a letter of enquiry and when the right man answered I paid him and his wife a call.

'Kamlesh came to stay with us about fifteen years ago. She can't have been much older than seventeen. It was during the time that my husband was stationed at the Red Fort in Old Delhi and we lived in a regimental cantonment near by. Although she was the daughter of my first cousin, I didn't know her well. She was a delightful girl, always smiling, and she had her baby with her, a little boy of about six months old. In fact I remember how fascinated she was by the old city here, especially the Muslim quarters, and she always enjoyed exploring the winding, narrow streets and alleyways. She would slip off with just the baby in her arms and wander for hours around the bazaars. She confided in me how she would take off her veil and nobody would take any notice of her.

'She'd been married for less than two years and she was already finding her married life constrained and claustrophobic. It wasn't at all what she had been used to, but then most Rajput girls feel like that when they first get married. Her husband, Padam Singh, seemed nice enough, not particularly bright, but his manners were good, and he seemed fond enough of her. They came at her suggestion. I think he wanted to apply for a post with my husband's regiment but his educational qualifications weren't up to standard. They must have stayed with us for about ten days. After they left I never heard another word from her.'

Mrs Bikram Singh and her husband, a colonel recently retired after forty years of service, lived in a recently constructed residential colony 10 miles east of Delhi. The news they heard of the depressed condition of Kamlesh came as no surprise to them. They knew the young woman's parents, although they were no longer

1 On my first visit to India I was delighted by the warmth and curiosity of the women   2 In the North Indian city of Patna, the women of the household prepare the meals

in touch. Colonel Singh remembered Kamlesh's father, a maharaja, very well.

'He was the grandson of one of Rajasthan's former most noble princes, Thakat Singh Oth. They lived in a small palace in Jodhpur – thick carpets throughout, bathrooms with hot and cold running water, all modern conveniences and luxuries including electricity and overhead fans. There were also family homes and estates in Madhya Pradesh and Simla. Despite all his land, gold and silver, he was completely uneducated. He never did a day's work in his life and certainly had no sense of responsibility. As a result he resorted to drinking and neglected his assets which gradually disappeared as he lived off capital. I first met him when I got married, over forty years ago, and at that time he must have owned at least half a dozen cars and employed a retinue of twenty servants. One year later he was down to only two cars. After that both these cars were in service as taxis in Jodhpur.

'He was a big landowner, too, and I remember that both he and his wife used to wear fabulous jewellery. For the first twenty years of their marriage they enjoyed a luxurious standard of living, even though his wife gave birth to another child almost every other year. Besides his complete inability to manage his affairs, the government's seizure of the privy purses of the old princedoms certainly contributed to his downfall. With so many daughters (I think there were about eight altogether) he would grab any opportunity to find them all husbands. The purity and nobility of a prospective husband's family tree were of greater importance than his economic standing and Kamlesh's in-laws are quite unable to supply any of the luxuries she was accustomed to as a child. Taking all things into consideration, I am not surprised that Kamlesh sometimes feels so unhappy. The difference between her childhood homes and the cattle farm in the desert where she now lives is incomparable.

'Many people tried to persuade the Maharaja to encourage all his children to study. His sons received a little education, but he never bothered about his daughters beyond having them taught the rudiments of reading and writing. Kamlesh was probably the brightest of the girls. The Maharaja was interested only in himself and the pleasures of alcohol, and his inebriety led directly to

3 I was dazzled by the brilliant dyes and colours worn by these Rajasthani women

Kamlesh's present situation. She is suffering now for the sins of her father.'

I was to discover that Kamlesh was as much the victim of tradition as unlucky in her marriage, and later conversations with her and her husband's family revealed that her personal sense of deprivation was only relative. All her six children were bright and though they lived in an area which was under threat of a severe drought they had always eaten well. Their home was sturdy and she was in good health. Very occasionally she had been beaten by her husband but then only when he had been drinking. Yet she was trapped by the way of life of her husband's family and the demands made on her by them and her children. Her own sisters' marriages were not so different from hers except they lived in closer proximity to one another and had been able to keep in touch. She also felt isolated because she was able to compare her childhood experiences to her present life. She knew another life existed and she could not block off the memories. It seemed as if she was the one doomed to suffer and there was nothing anyone could do to help her.

Six months after my first introduction I returned to talk to Bhawar Singh and his family. I was welcomed as an old friend, the women lifted their veils and I was implored to share their food and even to spend the night. At first they expressed mirth at my inquisitiveness, then they began to enjoy answering my questions, curious to know how their life differed from rural life in Europe.

Bhawar Singh was in his mid-seventies. Over twenty years earlier he had retired as a second-class magistrate to manage his inherited land. He had then purchased the present home, Manapia, set in 500 acres of arid scrubland. The bulk of his livestock was made up of oxen and sheep. Bhawar had little control over the grazing pastures when years passed by with little or no rain at all, but there had always been sufficient water in this desert outpost to supply the homestead. He had built a dam to preserve what little rainfall there was, but even when the reservoir dried out they had only to dig down 15 feet into the sand to find a fresh supply pure and safe enough for human consumption.

For up to ten months in the year Bhawar lived and worked on his farm with his wife Antarkanwar, son Padam, daughter-in-law

Kamlesh, five grandsons and one granddaughter. The only crop they could raise on the sand was black millet which, when reaped, they kept for their own use, feeding the stalks to the cattle. Should the rains be uncharacteristically plentiful, they attempted to grow some wheat. They kept a few goats, using the milk for curd, and from their cows' milk they made their own ghee (clarified butter). The remaining two months, during the cold winter weather when biting winds in the desert can cut and chap hands and faces, they spent in a small town house in Jaisalmer. Bhawar's family originally came from Khuri, some 20 miles from Manapia. He still owned 100 acres there, land inherited from his father which would eventually pass to his grandsons, but the land was unfit for cultivation and therefore of little value.

Manapia was 3 miles south of the main road which wound across the desert towards the border of Pakistan and the former empire of Sindh. Returning to the farm from Jaisalmer, the Singh family would travel by bus or pick up a passing jeep. A sign on the road warned drivers, 'Your hurry may cause others worry.' Then they would either walk or, if possible, arrange for their cowherd to meet them with a camel.

Bhawar had built his house eight years earlier with stone taken from a ditch below the dam and cement brought from Jaisalmer by camel. It was a handsome and sturdy construction with two rooms, a walled courtyard and a large circular room for cooking and eating. The portals and attractive carved wooden doors were also transported from the city. The main living area had a solid roof of timber frames, made from the roida tree, notable for its beautiful yellow blossom, plastered over with a mixture of clay, sand and cement. To allow ventilation, the kitchen was enclosed with a thatched roof made of grass which had become very brittle and dry, and kept breaking off and falling into the cooking pots. It was doubtful whether it would withstand the rains which were necessary to nurture the growth of new grass to replace it. The interior temperature was always cool, even in the summer months when hot sands were blown about all through the day and the temperatures soared as high as 45°C.

A primitive drainage system surrounded the homestead but it was quite inadequate during a heavy downpour. However, with light showers so rare, a heavy rainfall was welcomed with joy and delight rather than concern about inefficient drains. A small room, built apart from the main section of the home, was set aside for travellers and guests who wished to stay overnight, as only female outsiders were allowed into the family courtyard. Although welcome at all times, visitors were infrequent, and Padam normally rested and slept there, away from the noise and demands of his younger children.

In today's market Bhawar's estate would be worth about 300,000 rupees (approximately £15,000, at 20 rupees to £1), but sale of property is regarded locally as a sign of weakness and failure on the part of the proprietor. In Rajput society, a man attaches great importance to other people's regard for him, and purchasing land and building a home is considered one of the finest acts a man can perform for his family.

The farm usually earned them 40,000 to 50,000 rupees a year, the sale of oxen accounting for half of that income. Fortunately, land tax was negligible, but they had to pay for the education of Padam's children and fed not only themselves but also the wives and children of their retainers, so there was little cash to spare, and certainly not enough to consider purchasing their own truck or tractor. Though it was possible to hire a tractor in Jaisalmer, they still tilled the land using a camel or a pair of oxen. When the agricultural yield threatened to be especially poor, Bhawar leased out a portion of the arable land in return for a half share of the crop.

They owned three camels, which have a useful working life of about twenty years. A healthy young beast could be purchased in the market in Jaisalmer for about 5,000 rupees. The cost of animals depended on their age and state of health and they would fetch a higher price when the monsoon was good. If the rains are scarce a prospective purchaser is unable to feed a new herd. In the market today an ox costs around 14,000 rupees; a horse 10,000; a cow 1,200; a sheep 300; a goat 250; and a young cockerel 75 rupees.

Bhawar employed a cowherdsman, Kim Singh, who was also a Rajput and for whom he had constructed a house alongside his own. Kim Singh shared his home with his brother who worked in Jaisalmer during the tourist season organising camel safaris. Alongside Kim Singh lived a family of Darogas.

12

The Darogas are another tribe belonging to the Kshatrya caste, with roots going back some two hundred years. It is believed that their forefathers were those born as the result of clandestine affairs of Rajput nobles. Invariably these offspring were incorporated into their biological father's family as domestic servants. In the past, a Daroga girl servant was frequently expected discreetly to give favours to her mistress's husband. A Daroga maid was part of the dowry of Bhawar's wife at their marriage, over forty years ago, and this same maid took care of Padam and Kamlesh's children, her own family living in a homestead some 40 yards from her employers. Bhawar complained that he spent as much on their wellbeing as he did on his own family. He even had to pay for their daughters' dowries and was responsible for making sure that none of them went hungry, although their contribution to looking after the household was minimal. Life in the desert was too claustrophobic and interdependent for one family to eat well while their neighbours starved. Today, many Daroga families, believing themselves to be historically racially more pure than their Rajput landlords, tend to feel jealous towards their employers. Their male members now find better jobs away from the small communities and with their new financial independence they drink and socialise in the local towns and often persuade their wives and mothers to revolt against what has sometimes been a hierarchical form of enforced bondage.

Bhawar knew that in the future giving a Daroga servant with marriage would present great problems. 'When my grandsons marry, should a bride's father offer a Daroga girl I will probably refuse. It creates unnecessary extra expense. She may sleep with a boy or she could run back to her father's house. Wealthy families still continue with the system but soon I think it will cease to exist.'

I was curious to find out who lived in the humble dwellings some 400 yards from the Darogas' home, as the women, who wore fabulous bracelets all up their arms and large rings in their noses, kept to themselves when they went to fetch water. They were a small community of Muslims, shepherds, occasionally employed by Bhawar. A couple of years earlier, they had built themselves small dwellings of wood and dried grass and installed their families. Despite their different religious customs, all the children on the estate

13

played happily together, although the women tended to keep their distance from one another. The local government had constructed a small schoolroom in the vicinity, and on three mornings each week a teacher visited to instruct the younger children in the basics of reading and writing. About fifteen children attended, some coming from neighbouring families of the Bhil tribes who traditionally worked as labourers and cattle tenders.

Bhawar observed how much the system of employing help had changed over the past few decades. 'If my father, when he was alive, needed to hire an extra cowherd, say, the labourer would bring his wife and children and sometimes even his parents to stay at the house, and instead of being paid for his services the whole family would be fed and clothed. If a daughter was married while her father was in service, my father would be expected to pay for the wedding feast. That system has completely changed. The people I employ want more freedom and choice, so as well as housing them and feeding their families I also have to pay a salary.'

When the monsoon failed, most of Bhawar's herd had to be led far away by two Muslim shepherds in search of grass and water. Twice the men returned 20 miles alone, saying they had to leave the poor starving animals behind to die. The cattle which remained at the homestead became so weak that they had to be carried to a watering spot.

At the time of my second visit, a severe drought was forecast for the region, maybe the worst in the area this century. The reservoir was dry but there was still water underground. Once a month two well-diggers came from the city. There was no particular formula for choosing where to dig, even though it took them a whole day. Bhawar always had a hunch and nine times out of ten he was right. He refused to think about the threatened shortage.

'There's no point in wasting useful energy worrying about something over which I have no control. The water we have now is so sweet it's like manna from heaven.'

Although there was a communal well a mile and a half away, Bhawar preferred to be self reliant. He planned to raise and extend his dam, and even to enlarge his herd. Such optimism gave him confidence, which in turn earned him great respect and admiration.

The idea of the marriage between Bhawar's only son, Padam, and Kamlesh had been put forward during a wedding in Jodhpur – always a good time to find suitable partners within the same clan. Kamlesh was fifteen years old, and in his anxiety to find husbands for all his girls her father jumped at the suggestion of an alliance, especially to a young man who was, in fact, distantly related. No matter the simplicity of the boy's background – better, maybe. A desert farmer may demand a decent dowry but he would never be in a position to press for payment. A sum of about 30,000 rupees was agreed but characteristically the Maharaja never fulfilled his obligations.

At the time the Maharaja was residing in his estate near Simla in the foothills of the Himalayas. In his wisdom Bhawar felt it would be unrealistic to bring Kamlesh from the comforts to which she was accustomed to the harshness of the desert where even the local dialect would be alien. However, family pressure prevailed and all seemed well when their horoscopes were matched. Bhawar recalled with pleasure the nuptial party setting off from Jaisalmer nearly two decades earlier. His party of twelve travelled to Chandighar via Delhi in a second-class railway coach and completed the journey by bus. It was the first time any of them had set eyes on a mountain and Bhawar was convinced they would fall over the edge as their vehicle wound round and round the hairpin bends.

'What an amazing and memorable journey it was. All around us high, high rocky hills and waterfalls!' he told me, lifting his arms in the air to show how large the mountains were.

Throughout the wedding ceremony Kamlesh's face was kept completely covered. Padam first set eyes on his bride's face when they were left alone together to consummate their marriage. As boys and girls in Rajput society never sleep together before marriage, he was more inclined to be curious about the rewards of physical intimacy than to worry about her beauty. How she looked was a lottery. What was going to be his prize in this 'lucky dip'? Not the first perhaps, but a good second. Although her face lacked a defined bone structure, Kamlesh's brown eyes were large and lovely and her wide mouth and generous lips broke readily into a warm and friendly smile.

We spoke together while she worked in the kitchen. She welcomed my company and the chance to talk about herself as she had kept

15

silent for so long and few people listened to her, let alone offered her sympathy in her plight.

'My memory is hazy about the impressions I had when I first met Padam on our wedding day. I just went through what was expected of me. I can't even say if things have turned out as I wanted, for I was only fifteen and hadn't really thought about such things. What I did miss at first was the social life. My parent's homes were so large, and there were always people coming and going. The new life in Jaisalmer and at Manapia was so quiet, and I myself hardly opened my mouth. I had grown up speaking Hindi and couldn't understand the local dialect of Marwar. Almost straight away I gave birth to a little boy, so I immersed myself in looking after him while the rest of the world went on around me unnoticed.'

Her eldest son, Ajendar, was sixteen years old. Her second son, Dalvir, was three years younger. He had contracted polio when he was a few months old, which had left him with a slight limp. Although he could not run fast he was perfectly able to walk long distances. Before the birth of each of her children, Kamlesh had worried about the child turning out to be a girl. She still had vivid memories of her own father bemoaning his lot, and she had heard how girls were often killed off by being fed opium at birth. She had been told that nearly all the population of a local village below fifteen years was male. Fortunately, she had given birth to a further three boys and just the one girl, Damianti, who, as the only daughter, was much beloved by all the family.

The first three children were born in the family house in Jaisalmer, delivered by a local midwife, while the last three were all breach and born at Manapia. 'Is there a moral there? Did those babies want to stay in the comfort of the womb rather than begin the long trek across the desert?'

Despite the complications of the last deliveries, childbirth was never difficult for her. Great care was always taken afterwards to restore her strength and she was immediately given traditional restorative remedies: ijma, a cooking herb which helped disperse the afterbirth, singura, which helped the hips and spine go back to their correct positions, resins for strength and ginger to clean out the system. Although her labours were easy, Kamlesh felt quite drained by giving birth, and her mother-in-law and the Daroga cared for the small children while she rested for a few weeks.

The elder sons were studying in Jaisalmer where they learnt to speak and write Hindi and a little English. They were also taught some history, geography and science. Traditionally, education has always been considered a priority for the sons of Rajputs. Bhawar paid 1,500 rupees annually in school fees for each grandson. Apart from the eldest (who will inherit the farm, practise agriculture and breed cattle) their parents' desire was for them to enter the army or the police force, or to work with the border security services or in government. Should they fail to achieve such positions, they would return to the land but in a subordinate role to the eldest son.

The little girl was also to be sent to school, for these days a basic education would enhance her chances of making a good marriage. As soon as her periods begin, her father will start looking for a suitable husband. Already she was encouraged to help her mother when she cooked, peeling garlic, onions and other vegetables. Her brothers never helped in the house, but Kim Singh showed them how to feed and milk the goats and cows.

Two years before I met the family, the third son, Richiraj, had excruciating pains in his left leg. As the boy also had a high fever which failed to respond to antibiotics, Bhawar persuaded Padam to take him by train to Jodhpur where tuberculosis of the bone was diagnosed, but nobody could suggest a cure. In time, the pain subsided, but, as Richiraj grows, the leg is withering and the joints are wearing out. Although nobody had told him that he would eventually be completely crippled, I sensed he knew by the pain reflected in his eyes and face. He was a handsome boy, the best looking of the five sons, with a shock of thick jet black hair and high cheekbones. His parents felt helpless. They didn't know who to consult, nor were they confident that any further attempt at getting treatment would prove successful, so they encouraged him to work hard at school in the hope that when he grew up he would get a good desk job with a good salary and thus be able to make a good marriage.

When looking for suitable partners for their sons, parents do not attach much importance to the personality of the girl. If her family is good, then they will accept the daughter. Things are changing, however. Bhawar believed that his grandsons would perhaps even want to meet the girl before accepting her. The custom of accepting a large dowry was diminishing too – the hardship involved for families attempting to meet these demands in today's circumstances being taken into account.

Neither Kamlesh nor Padam was openly affectionate with the children. It was their grandmother who hugged them most. As three-year-old Mahender tripped and cut his lip he instinctively turned to his mother. In exhausted irritation she passed him to the old Daroga servant who comforted and caressed him, and gently bathed his bleeding face. Padam protested that they had to be strict with them to counteract the old women's indulgence – 'Look how well behaved they are. It's all due to the order I instil in them!' – but in truth their father spent little time at the farm. During the holidays the children ran wild in the desert, playing kabardi, a version of tag, or khoka, similar to musical chairs, or persuaded Kim Singh to saddle up one of the family's three camels to take them for a ride. Their grandfather mused that young children led a very free and indulged life compared with how he was treated in his youth.

Bhawar Singh's ancestors had always, as their means permitted, adhered to a traditional way of life. Many of these traditions were admirable: to a Rajput, material comforts were of little value. What was in his blood was what mattered. Strong blood made him walk tall. A Rajput living in an urban environment would often joke about his cattle farming cousin: 'A person who eats wheat should know the difference between right and wrong. Animals eat only grass and weeds, hence their lack of perception and knowledge. So Rajputs living in the desert and denied a regular diet of grain often suffer from an impaired intelligence!'

Bhawar was proud of his ancestry, proud too to be a member of the warrior caste: 'In Rajasthan the local princes appointed our forefathers to protect their lands from possible invasion from the west and to administer justice within their municipality. We were their guardians. Some of us were Jagidhars, similar to barons in Europe, and had our own lands. Poorer members of our community tended the princes' sheep and cattle. Whatever our economic status today, we have a long and strong tradition of sharing among ourselves, and that still continues.'

Of all caste Hindus, Rajputs are the least concerned with concepts of physical 'pollution' and sexual morals. Their main characteristics are their qualities of pride and honour. A Rajput's word is absolute and within his community he exercises great generosity. If a Rajput farmer has no use for some of his land, he will happily allow a fellow Rajput to graze his cattle without expecting any financial return. The consumption of meat is a regular feature of the Rajput diet, and drinking whisky (known locally as English wine), and sharing a hookah of opium or tobacco is a sign of brotherhood and friendship.

Unlike other castes, Rajputs have always maintained good relations with Muslims, even after Partition. When Pakistan threatened to attack, they all joined forces with the family of the local maharaja and prepared a united self defence.

The position of females in traditional Rajput families is still very constricted, theirs being a deeply patriarchal society. From puberty a girl is expected to keep her face covered in male company (apart from that of her own father and brothers) and in the presence of older women, in order to attain a peaceful and harmonious life through commanding respect. They feel that when people become too open they lose regard for each other. Secrets have an unaccountable value which they lose when they are revealed. As soon as a Rajput girl marries, her husband and parents-in-law control her every movement. Only years later, when she herself has daughters-in-law, will she be able to exercise any control over her own family and their actions. Even a young man has to gain permission from his elders for what he can and cannot do. The eldest man's authority over the household is absolute. For this reason Kamlesh kept herself as distanced as possible from Bhawar, her face covered at all times in his presence. Inevitably this continual conduct of respect was exhausting and the will of a woman to live to old age is rare. Once she has fulfilled her duties as a mother and all her children are married there is little to live for.

Kamlesh had been barely a teenager when her periods started. Each month she had had to stay in her bedroom for seven days with the curtains tightly drawn. She wasn't allowed to appear before the sun and was forbidden to set eyes on all male members of the family.

But now being the only member of the household who could cook, she ignored the old taboos. If she didn't prepare the food everyone would go hungry.

Bhawar was not unaware of the evil of some of the old customs, and he deplored marriage as a means of enlarging one's wealth, regarding the arranged alliance as a way of attaining a bride with a good character. He did not treat Antarkanwar as a typical Rajput wife. She had developed a deep affection for her grandchildren, and for her husband too, though she tended to distance herself from him.

One evening as the light was falling the young children nestled beside their grandmother as she told them her favourite cautionary tale.

'One day the Devil knocked on my great-great-grandfather's door.

'"What do you want?" asked the Devil.

'"I want to know everything there is to know. The past, the present, and what is in store for me in the future." The man wanted complete knowledge.

'"Anything else?" queried the Devil.

'"No, that's all."

'"That's all right but I think you're making a big mistake. However I'll grant it to you on one condition. What you know you will never reveal to anyone else. The day you do, you will go mad."

'"Agreed," nodded the man.

'One day as he was praying there was a bang on the door outside the fort where he was stationed. He could see a cluster of soldiers preparing their evening meal and with his new powers of perception and knowledge he saw a poisonous snake fall into their cooking pot unbeknownst to them. He realised that if the men ate the food they were preparing they would die. If he warned them they would want to know how he knew yet if he revealed what he knew he would be breaking his oath and would go mad. However, with his Rajput sense of chivalry, he decided he couldn't let them die and so he *did* warn them. Accordingly they were curious as to how he had this knowledge and challenged him. At his reply they fed a spoonful of the soup to a passing dog which promptly dropped down dead, and on emptying out the pot they found the skeleton of the snake –

whereupon my great-great-grandfather did indeed lose his head. So what is the moral of the tale? When a man passes on wisdom unasked for he is only creating problems for himself.'

For fifteen years from 1935, Bhawar was a Hakim, a legal representative of the local government. His duties in the service of the state included collecting tax and land revenues and acting as magistrate in minor criminal and civil cases.

'At that time the ruling Maharaja made us responsible for five or six villages. We had to keep in touch with all land and legal transactions. Landlords relied on us to sort out any disputes.' In 1950, when the state of Jaisalmer was incorporated into the state of Rajasthan, he continued working as a revenue inspector. He found it difficult to adapt to the new regime, working under District Collectors, so when his eyesight started to fail he applied for early retirement. He had few regrets as he had always wanted to spend time on his land and today he still receives a state pension of 200 rupees per month.

'Maybe I had been spoilt. Life was good and just during the time of British Rule. There were no local disturbances. The Maharaja had his own power, the Jagidhars, or landlords, and the Hakims had theirs. Everybody ruled and governed in a fair way. We would say that the tiger and the goat could graze together. If anyone had a problem with the Hakim, he would consult the Maharaja. If the Maharaja was unable to sort it out, he would contact the official representative of the British Government stationed at Mount Abu and his decision and judgment was always fair and good.

'I shall always remember the rule of the Maharajas in Jaisalmer, the families of Jawar Singh who reigned supreme from 1914 to 1949. Jawar Singh was the nephew of my grandfather so I had a special regard for his family.' Although his son, Padam, often wore a vividly coloured turban, Bhawar always wore one in a plain and pale colour. 'This is always the way in our family. When one of us passes away we forgo wearing bright patterned clothing. Although I was only distantly related to the Maharaja I wanted to make my own gesture of affection. I have such good memories of the fine times I had working in his service. Everyone was so prosperous and happy. Life will never be like that again. I know those halcyon days are gone for ever. Everything was cheap. One rupee would buy 50 grams of silver and 10 grams of gold cost 21 rupees. Today's price is 2,400 rupees! Whichever way a man turns now, corruption and greed prevail. Fair justice is a thing of the past.'

He found it difficult to support the current government and disliked the reservationist system introduced to forward the social mobility of the backward classes (those at the bottom of the caste hierarchy) and scheduled castes (those outside the system altogether).

'Even if one of my grandsons graduates with good certificates, when he seeks a particular post he will be discriminated against because he is a Rajput. They will tell him that on their job quota there is no provision for him but then an ignorant Harijan will get selected. Surely this is wrong? The favours should be granted to those with good education.

'During my lifetime I have had plenty of gold and silver. I gave fifty tolas [550 grams] when my only daughter got married and I had to part with one lakh [100,000] rupees' worth of gold and silver. When her two daughters married I gave them forty thousand rupees each. Now all I have left is eighty to ninety tolas of gold. [One tola of gold today is valued at 2,500 rupees – so his total value of remaining gold is worth approximately 2 lakh rupees, circa £10,000.] I keep the gold and silver coins and the silver ornaments buried. Very few family members know where they are although some of the jewellery occasionally worn by my wife and Kamlesh is kept in a locked box in the store room.

'One knows there is progress in another world, advances in medicine, new materials, terylenes and the like, but all these comforts and privileges have been gained at a cost to others, usually those already without.'

At forty, Padam had much less to show for himself in terms of worldly advancement than his father, Bhawar. For a short period he was a truck driver, but he gave it up because he felt the occupation to be too demeaning for someone of his social status. He worked briefly with Central Information in Jaisalmer, where he was expected to keep abreast of political manoeuvres concerning the land bordering Pakistan. It is an extremely sensitive area and the local authority has always had to be vigilant in order to prevent undesirables from coming across the border. Unable to apply himself to the job with the necessary vigour and efficiency, Padam was forced to resign, although honour prevented him from admitting to dismissal. He claimed to have left in order to take up family responsibilities on the land. But as long as Bhawar was physically active Padam would have to play second fiddle, and so he spent his days in Jaisalmer, drinking and smoking opium in the company of other idle friends. With relish he consumed kasturi, a saffron liqueur brewed locally, unaware that, like so many Rajputs of younger generations, he was relying on the efforts of his father for stability while he was becoming more and more dependent on alcohol.

Every time I went out to Manapia, Padam would insist on accompanying me back to my hotel where he would seek out company and order himself a beer. He was always courteous and friendly to me and in time I came to like him. I could see that he got bored at the farm. He showed no desire to play with his younger children and unlike his father he wasn't really interested in caring for the livestock. On one visit he collected me himself, driving an old battered van which he had borrowed from a friend. For three days he had operated a taxi service, collecting tourists from the station. Although he only spoke a few words of English he enjoyed showing foreigners around his home town. For once, it made him feel important, increasing his self respect, and out of the eye of his watchful parents he felt a sense of release.

Bhawar was not blind to his only son's shortcomings. He knew he had a weak character and was vulnerable to the corruption of city habits. 'I don't like his drinking but he is of an age now to have to take responsibility for his own actions. However, as a son, he has always obeyed me and in my company he does what I say. Whatever he does when I am not around he keeps to himself, and I don't think it is my business to interfere.'

Although Bhawar was loyal towards his son, he still found it difficult to come to terms with Padam's lack of direction. 'When he left government service he told me that he didn't want to be transferred to another state. That was the reason he gave me for leaving his job. He said that, as my only son, it was his duty to look after his parents, but I think his mind was disturbed at the time. Now I find it heartbreaking to watch him. All day he sits idle and is unable to assist me and Kim Singh with the estate. When I am gone he will have to face life's problems on his own. It will be difficult enough. Let us hope he is not hampered by an addiction to alcohol. Sometimes I doubt the wisdom in my educating him. He now regards himself as superior to the problems of recycling camel and cow dung.'

Yet Padam stated emphatically that he was quite happy with the way his life was ordered. I had no doubt that he enjoyed the freedom allowed him while his father was still taking responsibility for family and estate matters, but he professed to a growing attachment to the farm at Manapia. In his father's earshot he said he was beginning to feel less the pull of city life, and could see the effect it had on people scrambling after so few jobs. On the farm there would always be something to do, and with the dam, unless they were disastrously hit by drought, there would always be water.

Although he was aware of the way he took advantage of his wife's role of devotion and servitude, he was oblivious to her real feelings of deprivation and isolation. And despite weaknesses in his own character he could be intolerant of those in other people. 'Truth is all. In my opinion that a man should be true to his word is of paramount importance. I am angered by people who make mistakes.'

Paradoxically Padam himself suffered from an inferiority complex. He could feel put down when in the company of those better off than himself both spiritually and financially. He knew he hadn't achieved a very high position in life, but in equal company he was ready to accept that things were not so bad.

Padam's mother, Antarkanwar, had only two children, and he was her only son, so naturally she was proud of him and would not believe stories of his dismissal from the Intelligence.

'He had an accident while riding his bicycle on duty and hurt his nose.' At this I had to suppress a smile. 'When my husband dies, he's going to have to take over the running of the family land and properties, so he shouldn't take avoidable risks.'

Antarkanwar's own father was a respected village Rajput farmer who employed a teacher to instruct his children in the basics of reading and writing. She conceded her ignorance of worldly matters, but she wrote regularly to her daughter who now lived at Pokaran, just

4 *A Rajasthani peasant*   5 *Communal bathing in a North Indian village*
6 *The Singh's homestead at Manapia*   7 *Bhawar Singh with his son Padam and eldest grandson*   8 *Kamlesh cooks in the airless kitchen*

off the main highway to Jodhpur. 'I've seen television a few times in a neighbour's house. I didn't think the programmes were very informative and I certainly wouldn't allow my son to purchase one for us. We maintain the house in Jaisalmer so that the children have somewhere to live while they're attending school, and a television would be detrimental to their studies.

'I know in many ways we are backward. I personally understand nothing of this modern world. There is only one man among us with real earning power, and he has to support us and all the children. Just how is it possible for him to carry us all on his shoulders? We are all a burden on him. It was much simpler when I was a young woman and our fathers were a part of the ruling community.'

She knew that it would be unthinkable for a Rajput woman even to stroll around the city, let alone work outside the home.

As a former Hakim and retired magistrate, Bhawar was approached for advice by families who were unable to settle their disputes and differences internally. Although he disliked staying in Jaisalmer (he considered time away from Manapia as time wasted), he was unable to disappoint his former clients. Recently he had been called to town by a neighbouring family which had offered a large dowry for a husband for their daughter. Negotiations between the families had proceeded smoothly and with goodwill at first, but then on meeting their prospective son-in-law it was discovered that he had a withered leg, and so the daughter was withdrawn from the match. The boy's family were outraged, claiming that his slight physical disability would in no way impede his future. Meanwhile the girl's family hurriedly arranged another union for her and offered the disappointed groom some small financial compensation. But his family wouldn't accept the money, and insisted that the girl's younger sister should marry their crippled son. Bhawar listened carefully to the presented case, thought awhile and made his suggestion. Surely it would be better to abandon the thought of marriage between the two families altogether? There would seem little point in proceeding with a union in an atmosphere of ill-will.

Despite his protests about spending time in the city, Bhawar had a great affection for the fort of Jaisalmer and the town itself. His own ancestors made many sacrifices to protect it from alien oppressors,

9 The Daroga servant decorates six-year-old Damianti's hand with a paste of henna and lime   10 Damianti enjoys a carefree childhood in the desert

and many of his relatives lived within its walls. He was wary about the presence of overseas tourists, and the effects their habits had on the local population, although he appreciated the jobs being created by camel safaris and that the government's attention had been alerted to the need to renovate and maintain the crumbling structure of the fort itself.

For Bhawar, life was a constant struggle between the traditional values and the need to come to terms with the modern ways. In his middle years he had been very much in control of his affairs but that grip was loosening. He was nostalgic about the past and apprehensive about the future. Where Rajputs had once felt so sure of their position in society, now there was a basic sense of insecurity. As with all high-caste Hindus who felt threatened by the recent social mobility of backward classes and scheduled castes, many Rajputs doggedly refused to alter or adapt to a more modern way of life. I perceived that the older generation should perhaps begin to accept that, although they themselves can't change, they could encourage their children to take a clearer look at the real world around them so that their situation does not continue to deteriorate.

As long as he was fit and could still see where he was going, Bhawar would continue to work. Every morning he rose long before dawn and took whatever cows and bullocks were still at the homestead in search of grazing land. During the hottest hours of the day he would find some shade and rest, waiting until it was cooler to start walking back home.

'Sometimes I supervise my workers. I am not so old. I am still as tough as an ox and my willpower and health are very strong, but my eyesight is weak and it can be difficult for me to make out where there is suitable pasture for the animals.'

If he anticipated the possibility of spending a night away from home, he would take some flour and onions and prepare himself a light meal of bhajias on a portable chula, a small metal stove. Otherwise Kamlesh would fill his tiffin can with rotis, dal and vegetable curry. About twice a week he shaved himself with an old cut-throat razor, and in Jaisalmer the barber would come to the house, but Bhawar was not bothered with these small details of his life. 'I don't drink tea, coffee or alcohol, nor do I smoke, although my wife does sometimes. She has some disease of the stomach, and someone told her that an occasional bidi would have a settling effect.'

No one else stirred before sunrise. Kamlesh was usually next to get up and immediately she started to clean the house. Before breakfast she brewed some tea – leaves, sugar and milk all stirred together in the pot. Then she prepared the first meal of the day, perhaps fried roti with the previous evening's remaining vegetables stirred into the dough, and a large bowl of delicious raita, a mixture of curd, onion, chilli, salt and turmeric. The family used plenty of turmeric in their diet for they believed in its medicinal qualities as an efficient disinfectant for the stomach. Kamlesh rarely ate breakfast herself. As soon as she had fed the children she started making curd for the midday meal, storing all the milk products in a large metal cage, safe from the cats and rats. She prepared all the family's food. Her mother-in-law helped to clean the house and courtyard despite severe arthritis preventing her from standing upright. The Daroga servant's young granddaughter, Leela, scooped up the dust and loose ends of straw with her hands, tipped them into a wide basket and emptied it just outside the entrance door. The little girl worked willingly, often singing and humming as she swept, cleared out the cattle shed, collected dung and cleaned the cooking pots.

One morning as I watched the outside yard being cleaned I jotted down the contents in my notebook. There were two large round water jugs with wooden lids; winnowing baskets and brushes stored above the grain store; and two charpoys (wood and rope bedframes) stacked upright against the walls during the daytime.

Before taking his breakfast, Padam washed his hands with sand and Leela held out a small brass pot of water in which to rinse them. He cleaned his teeth with a Western-style toothbrush and toothpaste. Then Leela refilled the brass pot and handed it to Padam who took it in his left hand and walked out of the courtyard to relieve himself, crouched behind a sand-dune. Water being scarce, the daily washing ritual observed in other parts of the country was carried out here at most twice a week. The grown men made a special trip to the well to wash there, but Kim Singh brought water up to the house for the women and children, collecting it in large leather pouches which he strapped to the back of a camel. There was a special bathing place alongside the spot where the calves and goats slept and ate.

The women did all the work in the home, as well as caring for the children and milking the goats. It is rare for a Rajput woman to do any work outside the confines of the homestead, so a man was always responsible for collecting water.

At night-time the children tended to curl up together on the kitchen floor when they felt tired. Before she retired herself, maybe as late as eleven o'clock, Kamlesh prepared their bedding in the main room and tucked them up on the ground beside their grandparents who had a charpoy each. Unless Padam wished to exercise his male rights, he and Kamlesh slept in the courtyard in the open air.

I was treated with great respect on the occasion I stayed the night. One of the charpoys, on which I laid out my sleeping bag, was brought into the living room for me. This particular visit was in the month of April when the nights were warm so there was no need to use the quilts and rugs which were kept folded in one corner. I was amused by all the other things which were kept there too – a 100-kilo sack of cowcake, one pair of large wellington boots (in dry weather they are worn at night when walking in the desert as a protection against snakes), three sacks of building cement, a radio, a sewing machine and a battery-operated clock which had broken.

Before I settled down for the night, Antarkanwar showed me into the store room alongside. Running along two walls was a decorated shelf modelled in Rajasthani clay latticework on which Kamlesh stored various personal trinkets, a small mirror, three small brass pots, plastic flowers, tins of coloured paints, a couple of old torches, empty plastic jars for storage and empty kerosene bottles. There were curd and milk pots and four tin trunks of clothes placed on wooden stools to protect the contents from rats. Resting on the trunks were five extra embroidered quilts for winter use and quilts used on the camels' saddles. Stacked in one corner on the floor were empty tin cans for kerosene, baby-milk powder, some Hindi school exercise books and a few of Kamlesh's romantic novels.

Antarkanwar used to do the cooking but when her son married she instructed her daughter-in-law how to prepare many different dishes. Theirs was a mixed diet of meat and vegetables. For hours

28

on end Kamlesh would crouch by her stove, chopping garlic, onions and vegetables, grinding chilli, sifting the grain of jowar (a type of wheat) and millet, and kneading the dough and rotis, while Leela and her mother kept the fire going with sticks and cakes of dung. Fortunately camel dung burned slowly – not creating too much smoke. Even though it was very dark, Kamlesh would often read while she cooked. Always there was an opened page of a romantic novel beside her in the dingy light as she sat beside the clay chula. Her sons brought books for her when they came home from their school in the city. The evening meal sometimes took her three hours to prepare. She had to make a variety of dishes for many people.

I always enjoyed sitting in the kitchen with Kamlesh. The calm atmosphere in the darkened hut emanated from the manner in which she applied herself to her tasks, her dignity and her gentle smile. While I watched her deftly chopping a root of fresh ginger into small cubes I made a list of the tools and equipment she used when cooking – four sharp knives; two brass bowls for lassi; ten clay cooking pots; five kerosene bottles; a large iron pan for frying roti; a wooden board and rolling pin; ten spoons for cooking and serving and a wooden spice box divided into six compartments for powdered chilli, cumin, marsala, turmeric, pepper and garlic cloves. Also in the kitchen were four brass beakers; three large brass dishes for guests; four aluminium plates; ten aluminium vegetable pots; four brass milking pots; a brass teapot for guests; four metal tea mugs and five metal water beakers.

Sometimes in the winter Kim Singh shot an imperial eagle, a large bird migrating from Siberia, whose flesh, though tough, could be tasty when marinated in spices and stewed with onions. Often they slaughtered their own goats, and they grew some grain and millet for themselves, the rest being brought in from Jaisalmer by camel. In the bazaar there they bought enough pulses and grain to last at least two months, and if there was enough cash they purchased as much as 125 kilos of grain at 2.50 rupees a kilo. About 600 rupees went every month on 25 kilos of sugar, and on chilli, tea and kerosene. Their own cows produced about 10 litres of milk every day, from which they prepared their own ghee and curd, and vegetables were obtained as they needed them.

A passing cattle or camel driver was treated as a guest and invited to take food with them. Often a feast was prepared – tomato curry, garlic pickle, ladies' fingers, onions in curd and lime, ghee ladled on to chapattis made from black millet, washed down with a beaker full of fresh lassi, cooled in a large earthenware pot.

Only traditional medicines were used for sickness. Anyone suffering from a bad head-cold or a fever would be given a special tea made with cardamom, black pepper, ginger and jasmin seed boiled in water until it was reduced to a thick potion. The brew was drunk before going to sleep under a thick quilt to work up a big sweat. By morning the cold or the fever would usually have disappeared. Despite her rheumatism and weak stomach, Antarkanwar liked to boast that she had no idea what the inside of a hospital looked like, and Padam said that he had never even seen a doctor. 'There's no need for that. I'm such a good sleeper that during the night my body restores itself.' None of them had ever visited a dentist. With plenty of calcium in their own milk products, their diet was good for their teeth despite the large quantities of sugar they consumed in tea. Chewing cloves to dull the pain was the usual cure for a bad toothache.

While the eldest boys were studying in Jaisalmer, and their father was often in the city drinking with his friends, it was a rare occasion for all the family to sleep together at the farm. Daily existence could be monotonous and uneventful. It was the seasons of the year, with the soaring heat and cold temperatures, which provided a little contrast to the pattern of their lives. For spring and harvest festivals, Dashera and Holi, all the family would gather to celebrate with days of feasting and music. I visited Manapia on the eve of the spring festival. When I arrived Grandma Antarkanwar was caressing and stroking the small children as they all laughed and sang songs together. As the evening light dimmed she sat on the doorstep of the living room smoking a bidi. The cattle were quiet and still; just one cricket chirped in the calm air. As soon as it was dark she stepped into the kitchen and watched Kamlesh prepare dinner. She crouched down and Damianti and Mahender, the youngest children, curled up beside her and fell asleep. The elder boys gazed in silence at the crackling flame under the stove while their mother prepared a vegetable curry. She had to lean over the flame, blowing at the embers of two wooden logs through a metal tube to create a steady heat. A strong gust of wind blew through the dried grass roof, shaking particles of dust into the cooking pot. There was just a dim light given off by the kerosene lamp hanging from the wall. As Padam entered the kitchen, Kamlesh pulled a yellow cotton veil down over her face. Already hampered by the dim light, she had to lift a corner of the veil as she reached out to select her ingredients. She was watched by all the family, but no one helped as she crossed the floor to sift the flour for the chapattis. She returned to squat by the stove, silently kneading the dough while the vegetables simmered.

Padam laughed quietly. 'What a thing it is, the duty of a Rajput wife, to feed all her family. It's a hard life!'

She served him first on a large aluminium dish with bowls of potato and pea curry, aubergine and tomatoes, spiced warm raita with cumin and raw onion and three hot crisp rotis fried in pure ghee. He ate with relish, washed his fingers with the remains of his drinking water, rinsed his mouth, gargled a little, let out a large belch and left the room to sleep in the guest house where there was a small bottle of whisky waiting under his pillow. As soon as he had gone, with relief Kamlesh lifted her veil. She could now feed the children without being hampered. As she prepared fresh chapattis the boys and their grandmother helped themselves directly from the cooking pots. Only when they were satisfied did Kamlesh herself eat, but after two hours crouched by the stove her appetite had waned.

Before each festival Kamlesh would go to Jaisalmer to organise new outfits for herself and the children. None of the women dressed in a conventional sari. Instead they wore a simple long skirt with short-sleeved blouse, sometimes choosing a floral pattern. They twined around their waists and shoulders a chiffon or thin cotton shawl in a matching colour. The material was purchased from a stallholder who brought a selection to the house and then a tailor was summoned to take their measurements. Apart from shirts for the men, they rarely wore ready-made garments. Occasionally Padam would put on a dhoti when he relaxed at home, but normally he dressed in Western-style trousers and shirts, with a woollen jersey during the winter. Only Bhawar used leather chappalls; all the others wore modern rubber thonged sandals on their feet.

Unlike other communities, the Rajputs' attitude to organised religion is more practical than spiritual, and they tend to adhere more to upholding the clan's traditions as warriors, protectors and landowners. Yet, like many Christians in the West today, at the time of a wedding or a death, they do on occasions turn to their own gods. The boys usually go through the sacred thread ceremony, an important Hindu initiation sacrament, shortly before marriage. Bhawar Singh's family deity was Jogmaya, an incarnation of Shiva, one of the three main Hindu gods, whose principal shrine is at Hardwar on the banks of the River Ganges, where he is worshipped in large ritual gatherings. His family had no special priest. When a birth was to be celebrated, or a marriage was being prepared, a priest was employed from one of the few Brahmin families still residing in the town.

Padam prayed irregularly, although every time he passed a small shrine on the main road he made a small gesture of respect. 'Religion is imposed by man. For me Hinduism is a way of life and a solace in death.' Yet he believed in rebirth. 'If I am devout I may be exonerated and arrive at my own personal nirvana [freedom from rebirth],' he said with a twinkle in his eye.

Bhawar said he prayed daily. 'I ask for spiritual pleasure and profit and to keep my thoughts good and free from evil thinking.' He believed in all the gods but personally prayed to the goddess Durga. As the earthly representative of power, many Rajputs offer their prayers to Durga, and in Jaisalmer she was often worshipped in her reincarnation of Marjantamba, Mother of the Universe. 'All Hindus believe in rebirth,' he stated emphatically. 'I know that if I conduct myself well in this life God will give me a good life again next time, but if I think "bad" thoughts I may be reborn as one of my animals.'

When a Rajput dies before his wife, she is subjected to a rigid ritual of mourning. She is expected to sit quietly for many months in a corner of the living room, sometimes hidden behind a curtain with her face completely covered. No other woman whose husband is still alive is allowed to see her face. Her only company, apart from her immediate family, is other widows. Her diet is kept to the bare minimum, just a little rice and water. She is not supposed to leave her position to relieve herself, a small pot being handed to her through the curtain. The clothes she wears for a specified time are of the same colour as those her husband wore when he actually expired. She takes no part in any of the elaborate funeral rites, although prior to the cremation she will take her farewell by walking backwards around his body. Twelve days after his death, all the widows in the neighbourhood come to lead her into the courtyard of her home where they ceremoniously smash the coloured wedding bangles she wears on her wrists and remove the gold pin from her nose. She is then dressed in black or white, the only colours she will wear for the rest of her days, and is led back to her position of isolation. For the rest of her life, she and her children will perform rituals and feasting on the anniversary of her husband's death. Both Bhawar and Antarkanwar remembered their own mothers being treated in this way, and Bhawar considered it inhuman that his mother, who had served her husband well and loyally, was confined to one room for the two years following his death.

Kamlesh occasionally said special prayers to Shiva. 'I pray, simply asking for salvation of my soul. What else is there to ask for now? Nothing can be changed. My responsibilities are complete. My children are growing up. It is their turn to make something of their lives. I just want some peaceful nirvana. There would be no point in repeating what I have already been through.'

She confided to me her feelings of frustration at what her life had become. 'What it is to marry a Rajput! His ego constantly has to be served. He does exactly as he pleases. Comes and goes when it suits him. I never know when to expect him but when he does show up he expects hot food, instantly, at any time of the day. Living here with only the Daroga women, whose general ignorance is so irritating, and the children and no other stimulation, it's driving me crazy. I've had some education but to me that doesn't only mean reading books. It's travelling, meeting people, many different kinds, so that one is able to exchange thoughts and ideas. Even though we have a guest house, people rarely stay. It's just somewhere for Padam to hibernate with his whisky.

'When I am in town I can never leave the house and go for a walk on my own. I have to ask my mother-in-law's permission for everything I do, yet it isn't she who makes the rules. We all have to bow to the wishes of my father-in-law. She may tell me what to do, how to cook and how to dress the children but her only aim is to please her own husband.

'But I know I am quite fortunate. In my heart I know that Padam is not a bad man. I think he would feel a lesser person if he treated me in any other way.'

Apart from their servants there was no one of her own generation to whom she could talk. If her parents had arranged for her to marry a boy from her home town she would have been able to stay in touch with her own sisters, or if Padam had a brother there would be some companionship for her from a sister-in-law. Kamlesh spent nearly every waking hour in the kitchen, preparing and cooking food, and often she slept there too, curled up beside the stove. Although she professed to be attached to her children, her maternal feelings had been dampened by her depressed state. A Rajput wife usually accepts her situation because she sees there is no way out. Such acceptance can be both a weakness and a modesty, a desire not to stand out or make any kind of vain show of herself while flinching at the knowledge that she may get hit very hard if she attempts to battle against her situation. In the end it is often more comfortable to keep a low profile and go along with the system. Despite the constrictions Kamlesh felt no urge to rebel. What would be the point of making trouble if it would change nothing? If she had refused to marry at the outset, she would have been made to feel by her own parents that she was causing great unhappiness for the rest of her family. Occasionally she sent them letters, but she rarely heard from them, and her husband would not allow her to travel to meet them. He was still angry because her father had failed to pay the promised dowry. It was impossible for her even to consider returning to her parents' home. Her father had managed his affairs so badly that he now lived in penury in a modest bungalow in Narsinghgarh, Madhya Pradesh, and he wouldn't encourage a visit in case she refused to return to her husband. Although she was still only thirty-three years of age, she considered the easiest way for her to complete her days was to fulfil her duty by being a good wife and to teach Damianti how to sew and cook so that she too would be well prepared for marriage. Educated Rajput women blamed the fifteenth-century lawgiver Manu for creating this and similar situations for wives in their community. He delivered the laws of social practice for Hindus and stated that women were defiled creatures.

Mrs Bikram Singh would not allow that Rajput tradition was to be blamed for her niece's plight. 'It is more a lack of education in her husband's parents. Her mother-in-law is so very dominant and insists that she spends all her time cooking and looking after the house so that she has no time at all for fun and games with her children. They need someone to play with but they will only be friendly with her if she gives some of her time to them. Nor is it a question of whether or not Padam is a good or bad man. He just doesn't know anything else except what he has seen in the narrow confines of his social life in Jaisalmer.'

Kamlesh remembered and took comfort from some wise words her aunt said to her right at the start of her marriage. '"Life is like a stream. Some days one feels bad and on others one can cope." I shall remember to tell my own daughter that when she grows up. If she sleeps on a problem, it will look different the next day. I know this is true. Every dawn and dusk a different light comes.'

Colonel Singh also pondered Kamlesh's situation, which he felt highlighted more than just the problems of women today. 'The deterioration of contemporary moral values has undermined the Rajput personality. In the past, when a Rajput made a promise, he kept it. They have always taken great pride in the honour of their word, so it is hard for them to comprehend the modern way. A man now says what will benefit him at the time regardless of whether or not he is telling the truth. The scheduled castes and tribes were far happier when they knew exactly where they stood with their landlords. Some of them may have good jobs but their welfare in general is no longer cared for. When you give a man everything, he becomes lazy. If he has to work for something he is a better person. Time and again, one maharaja works hard, his son then inherits and is lazy, squandering all his assets, and then in turn his son sees how his father's sloth affects the family so he becomes hardworking like his grandfather. Similarly, reward a Harijan with a fourth-class pass with a job on a par with a Brahmin with a first-class pass and his personality will become warped. A man needs education, honesty,

sacrifice and a lack of greed for a good and purposeful life. When I was at school each day began with a prayer. There was a desire to be helpful, truthful and not to be afraid. We were told that life isn't all earning money, cheating and drinking, but that there were moral principles which applied equally to all religions and castes.'

He was sympathetic, too, to the plight of Kamlesh's young husband. 'It isn't easy for Rajputs attempting to adapt to the new ways. They see a whole new type of person acquiring wealth and position overnight. How can they manage life today on a social level? Chivalry in their community is an inbred way of life for them, as is bravery and a sense of sacrifice. This only makes Padam's sense of failure more poignant. Today's desire is to rise within society with no consideration for those around one, upsetting the old Rajput tradition of caring for servants, feeding them, clothing them, providing them with land to cultivate. It is the sons of these servants who now have turned on their old masters, dominating them with a totally immoral code of behaviour.'

Despite his advanced years and his failing sight, the old cattle farmer Bhawar doggedly refused to let modern life blight his outlook on life in general.

'I am attempting to look to the future so that I can best advise my grandsons how to carry on the family traditions.'

3
Hinduism and
Caste

Before I met more families I realised that I was going to have to find out more about their religion and understand some of the basic concepts of their social system if I was to comprehend the culture and attitudes that I was beginning to see were profoundly different from my own. It was to prove a formidable task.

Although divided from the rest of Asia by the highest mountain range in the world, the Himalayas, the subcontinent of India has been invaded by many migrating tribes and races. Few records of these people, unlike those of the early Europeans, have survived. Such monuments that they had were built of wood and many were destroyed during the twelfth century A.D. by Muslims who invaded the country from the north-west. The rest have been damaged by centuries of drought and flood.

Since Hindus are not greatly interested in charting their own historical progress, the emergence of the Hindu religion is, in part, a matter of conjecture. It is thought that prior to an invasion by the Aryans around 1500 B.C. the original inhabitants of the Gangetic Plain (formerly known as the Indus Valley, from which developed the names 'India' and 'Hindu') were the Dravidians. They were a dark, mongoloid race, not dissimilar to the Australian aborigine in stature and in strength. It was the Muslims who named the inhabitants of the 'land beyond the Indus River', both Dravidians and Aryans, Hindus.

Today fewer than 20 per cent of India's inhabitants adhere to other religious traditions, namely Islam, Sikhism, Buddhism, Jainism and Christianity, so the vast majority of Indians are Hindus. But, unlike these other religions, outside India Hinduism is only found in countries where Hindus have migrated.

It is often said that the subcontinent of India is the most spiritual place in the world. It is the birthplace of Buddhism, the home of nearly 100 million practising Muslims and the motherland of Hinduism. My examination of the significance to a contemporary Hindu of his religion and its effect on the curriculum of his existence, although simplistic, may help to show an individual's sense of personal identity and moral survival within a society that continually confounded me with its rituals and customs. It is true that in recent years economic need and whirlwind advances in communication technology have eaten away at many Hindu beliefs, yet family unity and, indeed, faith remain dominant forces in most people's daily life.

Shortly after the Aryan invasions, around 1500 B.C., came the emergence of the four *Vedas,* collections of sacred hymns which were originally preserved by word of mouth, and from which evolved some of the ideologies of Hinduism. These hymns are in many ways simply a celebration of the wonder of the world in which man lives. Hindus have always been primarily concerned with the relationship between man and the universe, the earthly and the spiritual body. The only factual information to be gleaned from the *Vedas* is that the early agriculturalists of the Indus Valley were governed by warriors, or protectors, and that there was a band of priests who prayed for growth and well being.

Around 1000 B.C. came the epic age, when mythological stories contained in the *Ramayana,* the *Mahabharata* and the *Upanishads* were first told. The last of these was akin to a philosophical lecture expanded through moral folk tales. Its central theme is the relationship between Brahma, the Supreme Being, and the Atman, the inner self or soul. Brahma, the omnipotent God and King, is seen as the eternal self in whom all beings exist and as the source of Samsara, the transience and change experienced throughout one's earthly existence. The *Mahabharata* and the *Ramayana* are today as important to Hindus as the *Holy Bible* is to Christians. Not only do they tell of war and adventure but they also carry a message of the power and triumph of good over evil. Many of the characters in the stories are the vast variety of gods and deities which have come to govern the faith of all devout Hindus. Throughout can be perceived the basic philosophy of the Hindu – that is, his paramount concern with the nature of the universe and his curiosity in finding a personal relationship with God. Included in the *Mahabharata* is the *Bhagavad Gita,* a sacred book of celestial songs allegedly inspired by a mystic dialogue between Lord Krishna and the warrior king, Arjuna. There are twenty-eight chapters of hymns and prayers in all, wherein are written all manner of ways for man to find himself at one with God. There are instructions and teachings on how to attain complete knowledge and self-realisation, how one should conduct one's prayers, how one should separate good from evil yet accept the presence of them both, and, perhaps most important, the foundation of all Hindu thought: how one should discriminate between one's inherent nature and the future of one's soul and how through each life man must do his duty within the social context in which he finds himself. Contained in the *Ramayana* and *Mahabharata* are imaginatively coloured tales of how life at that time was conducted, with numerous clans, each functioning within its own unit.

Around 300 B.C. the *Puranas* were composed. These are historical documents of the mythical laws, intended to support the philosophies of the *Vedas,* and they include an exposition of the creation of the world, the concept of time and details of mythical kings. Concurrently a Hindu sage named Manu qualified various customs and religions and social duties in what is known as 'Manu's code'. This has been passed on through generations, and is followed today for the ways in which fasts and festivals should be observed.

At the outset Hinduism was a monotheistic religion whereby the one Supreme Being, Brahma, was worshipped. Under the umbrella of this omnipresent God, it developed into a polytheistic religion – one with many gods. There are three main physical representations, a triumvirate not unlike the Christian God the Father, God the Son and God the Holy Ghost. There is Brahma, the Godhead and Creator, Vishnu, the preserver of life, and Shiva, the destroyer. One cannot say that the Godhead is either male or female because it has many manifestations, and can be worshipped as a father or as a mother or even as a friend should one so wish.

Today Brahma is worshipped directly by a comparative handful of Hindus while Shiva, in various forms, has many worshippers. True, he destroys, but in destruction there is regeneration or transmigration, the passage of the soul at death into another body, and in transmigration there is hope. The most popular god is Vishnu, the kind and gentle one. He can be identified with living man, inspiring confidence, devotion and love.

Within India, the practice of Hinduism varies considerably from one region to another, indeed even from village to village, where there are considerable differences in the deities worshipped, the scriptures sung, festivals celebrated. And yet, although there are many variations under the umbrella of Hinduism, most Hindus will agree on the basic concepts.

First, there is the ancient belief that Truth and God are one. Second, there is the belief in the Atman, the inner soul of each individual, and, third, that behaviour in a previous life is responsible for the present condition. Everyone is stuck in a wheel, some form of circumventive pattern. A person's behaviour is a form of response to being encased in this fusion of infrastructure. The wheel turns continuously but one is free to detach oneself at will while at the same time retaining roots within. One should love one's neighbour as oneself but before one can do this one must come to a greater understanding of oneself and all human nature. Interwoven, too, in this wheel is one's dharma, the acceptance of the existence in which one finds oneself. 'I think, therefore I am, but what I am God knows.'

A Hindu's ultimate aim is to be freed from his Samsara (his earthly existence of change), and his soul liberated so that finally it achieves the ultimate Brahma—Atman relationship from which salvation comes. In practical daily life, purity of spirit and complete knowledge can be attained through the techniques of yoga, which enable one to achieve detachment from this earth and blessedness through union with Brahma. A devout Hindu must aim for the higher region of being, that of contemplation, rather than the lower region of possession.

The doctrine of the law of karma, by which every action has its appropriate result and justice is meted out for the reward or punishment of every action, is linked to the notion of the transmigration of souls. It is stated in the *Upanishads* that, 'Those whose conduct on earth has given pleasure can hope to enter a pleasant womb, that is, the womb of a Brahmin or a woman of the princely class. But those whose conduct on earth has been foul can expect to enter a foul and stinking womb, that is, the womb of a bitch or a pig or an outcaste.' This concept of rebirth is fundamental to the acceptance by many contemporary Indians of a miserable and unchangeable existence, and it explains why political reform in India through revolution is such a remote possibility. If a man suffers, it is his punishment for misdeeds in a former life, the penalty for breaking the codes of Hindu behaviour and not the fault of a corrupt system.

In times past, Westerners have inspected Indian traditions because they were thought to supply some kind of answer to man's destiny; religious philosophers continually asked, 'What is the destiny of man? Is he going to be consumed by the fire of death and mortality?' They have been fascinated by Hindus' enquiry into the unconscious chambers of the mind.

Hinduism is an eternal quest for knowledge and the Hindu philosopher's duty is to encourage his pupils to live in a state of eternal present and a oneness with the soul. There are many different ways of achieving this – it is not necessary to retire to an ashram in the Himalayas. Some choose intense devotion to God or continuous self-analysis and the pursuit of wisdom. Others prefer to work constantly and tirelessly in the way preferred by Mahatma Gandhi.

Hinduism is also a way of life. To the orthodox Hindu there are rituals to accompany every single action from the moment of birth, through childhood, maturity, old age and, finally, death – how one should wash oneself, whom one should marry, the food one can eat. Rituals are the soul of all cultures and the basic art of religion. Within Hinduism they can be so complicated that even a learned pandit, a priest and teacher, would have to devote his lifetime to master them.

The chief daily ritual that contemporary Hindus now observe is prayer, puja, an essential part of which is arti, the lighting of a small fire while chanting mantras. Fire gives out energy, its flames destroy evil. Throughout puja the mystic invocation of 'om . . . om . . . om' is hummed, a password for making contact with God. Moreover, the vibration of this repeated single syllable induces a state of inner peace. At the conclusion of puja, the prayer leader will press a bright vermilion dot mixed with grains of uncooked rice on to everyone's forehead. This ancient symbol represents a third eye which seeks out and detects on behalf of the bearers any evil they may encounter.

To high-caste Hindus, (the order of castes will be explained later in this chapter), the most important sacrament is the sacred thread ceremony. This section of society refer to themselves as 'twice born' – rather like birds, which are given an earthly form when their mother lays her eggs and then emerge again when they hatch. A Hindu boy's first birth is at his delivery and his second at this ceremony of initiation. This may take place any time after he has completed his sixth year. The thread is looped like a sash around his left shoulder and right side of his waist. It is a sign of an élite membership. The orthodox Hindu boy will then begin to learn and recite daily the Sanskrit verses of the holy texts.

The ancient Egyptian science of astrology, now discarded in the West, plays a significant role in advising Hindus on auspicious times for celebrations and festivals, for choosing marriage partners or a particular name, and for reading horoscopes. Rumour has it that in 1947 when it was announced that Independence from the British would take place at midnight on Friday 15 August, a learned Bengali pandit immediately inspected a large, circular chart on which the days and months of the year were placed within the cycles of the position of the sun, moon, planets, Zodiac signs and the stars. The relationship between the dates and the cycles influenced the earth's destiny. He was horrified to deduce the many conflictions occurring at this time and date, unfortunately correctly forecasting the ensuing disaster in which millions suffered untold misery when Muslims and Hindus were forcibly uprooted and repatriated into two separate nations.

Every village in India has its own special god, and shrines and altars line the highways throughout the country. Trees, rivers and cities are all sanctified by the past visitation of a favourite god. In India, the gods are invoked everywhere – in houses, on doorsteps, even on the pavements, often by means of exquisite drawings in coloured chalks, each containing a religious message within the intricate lines. Each home has its own domestic deity in the form of a small idol of pottery, brass or stone, which is sometimes treated like an errant pet from which offerings are withheld if a prayer is left unanswered.

Each god is associated with an animal, his personal conveyor, and also has a consort and children, who in turn have their own attributes and nuances of personality. For instance, Shiva rides on a bull named Nandi. He has two children, Kartikkaya, the god of War, and Ganesh, the elephant-headed god of prosperity and wisdom whose vehicle is, surprisingly, a rat. The popular family goddess Durga is second wife or consort of Shiva, and is an example of how one deity may also take on many guises or incarnations; when known as Parvati, she is a queen, a daughter of the glorious Himalayas, and as such is a driving female influence behind many other gods, enforcing upon them her gentle qualities of tenderness and love; as a mother she is always portrayed protecting her children, and this other side of her personality is naturally reserved, tending to make it difficult to become closely acquainted with her.

Another popular deity is Lakshmi, the consort of Vishnu. She is the goddess of wealth, fortune, power and beauty. To her is ascribed influence over fertility, production of water and prosperous agriculture. She is enchantingly beautiful and is often depicted standing on a lotus and holding two more, flanked by two elephants who pour pitchers of water over her. Her four hands signify her attributes of righteousness, wealth, pleasures of the flesh and beauty. Sometimes her vehicle is Brahma depicted as an owl, an incarnation of the king of gods and a symbol of wisdom.

The importance attached to the role of the gods in every aspect of the lives of Hindus should be appreciated, although a Westerner like myself can be surprised by so much money being spent on festivals when people are unable to feed their own children. However desperate a man's poverty, his taste for celebration is a visible expression of his own optimism.

Like Hinduism, the origins of caste are obscure. The earliest Hindus, who inhabited the area now known as the Punjab, included

Persians and Greeks who in the years B.C. steadily invaded from Central Asia. These northern Aryans pushed the Dravidian inhabitants southwards, and it is believed that caste divisions may first have come about when the original population was incorporated into the conquerors' new civilisation in a servile form known as Sudra. Although the Dravidians protested they were good Hindus, they were excluded from the 'twice born' theory and forbidden to practise the same sacred rites. Today, Sudras, or Backward Classes, the name by which they are officially known, account for nearly a third of the entire population of India.

There is a reference contained in the *Rig Veda* (*c.* 1200–900 B.C.), the first time the concept of caste is recorded in the history of Indian civilisation, which suggests a second theory of caste origins, namely that the system was formed within a group of families claiming common descent from Brahma, the mythical forefather. Initially the father was the Brahmin, the priest and teacher, the brother the warrior and protector, the sister the keeper of the household, and so on. However, after a few generations such organisation became impossible to perpetuate so groups of individuals with the same roles drew apart into separate guilds or castes.

There is a third theory contained in a delightful myth similar to the story of Noah wherein a celebrated man called Mahanuvu, greatly respected by all Hindus, escaped the great flood in his own ark taking with him seven famous Penitents. When the waters subsided they set about dividing mankind into four different castes.

The fourth theory of caste origin can be attributed to a reference in the *Bhagavad Gita* (ch. iv, v. 13) to the words of Brahma: 'The four castes were created by Me according to differences in aptitudes and actions of Men. Though I am its creator, know Me to be incapable of action or change.' Philosophers studying this work believe that the reasoning behind caste has an emphasis on gunja (aptitude) and karma (function) but not jati (birth and subcaste). The design of the embryonic caste system was thus based on man's inherent nature – each and every one of us possesses three main characteristics: pure qualities (meditative and contemplative), active qualities (the need to work and desire to participate and contribute) and qualities of inertia and lethargy (a lack of both willingness to utilise the mind and intellectual conceptions). Social position, jati, is then dictated by these characteristics.

Whatever the exact origin, by the fourth century B.C. the system was firmly entrenched, and the theory that the castes, the four Varna, issued from the one almighty deity, Brahma, is the most generally acknowledged:

From Brahma's mouth came the Brahmin, assigned special powers of divinity and the six duties of responsibilities of study, teaching, sacrifice, assisting others in their sacrificial duties, giving alms and receiving gifts for their priestly services. Today, many Brahmins still maintain their role as preacher and teacher.

From his arms came the Kshatrya, assigned the qualities of strength and the duties of studying, sacrifice, giving alms, acquainting themselves with the use of weapons, and protecting treasure and life so that good government can be assured. Today many join the army and the police force, or become rich and influential landlords. The Rajputs are one of the most powerful subcastes.

From his thighs came the Vayshya, assigned the duties of work, study, giving alms, cultivation, trading and tending cattle. Today they are businessmen, money lenders and landowners. The affluent Marwaris belong to this group.

From his feet came the Sudra, their duty being to serve the three higher castes. Today they are broken up into thousands of subcastes with specific roles, such as carpenters, blacksmiths, weavers, shepherds, toddy tappers (whose job it is to scale the tall toddy palm to extract the pungent liquor from within the tree), potters, dhobis (washermen) and many others.

The relationship between the Brahmin and the Kshatrya castes emerged quite distinctly as that between priesthood and royalty, not dissimilar to the link formed between the monarchs of England and the archbishops of Canterbury. Today, many Kshatrya subcastes believe that their forefathers were noble or princely. It seems, too, that there was cunning and logic behind the Brahmins allowing so much power into the hands of the Kshatrya. They sensed that by delegating to the Rajputs the responsibility of maintaining law and order, they would always retain their superiority as spiritual leaders. Although the Kshatryas are higher in status than the Vayshya group, more commonly known in India today as Banya, they are far less concerned by the caste conceptions of prayer and beliefs about food. Rajputs are well known for their enjoyment of consumption of all kinds of flesh, especially the wild game which they take great pleasure in hunting.

What has probably prevented a revolt against the caste system is the notion that caste was divinely ordained. However it is not a religion even though Hinduism and caste are interdependent on one another. Nor is it an occupation even though each subcaste is linked to a particular skill, agriculture in varying forms being the most widespread occupation in all castes.

Until the beginning of this century the following features dominated caste thinking: hierarchy – the strict ranking of families; endogamy – arranged marriages between partners within the same group (or occasionally hypergamy, when a bride could be taken from a slightly lower order); instructing one's offspring in one's own technical skills; customs over the consumption of food and drink; customs of dress; concepts regarding the notion of 'pollution'; the performance of rituals; caste organisation – the way in which each group conduct themselves within their own community; and, finally, caste mobility – the extent to which one can socialise outside one's caste. The first four practices, with certain modifications, still go on today in most rural areas, whereas attention to the others has greatly relaxed and in some instances disappeared altogether.

As the rules and routines practised by a devout Hindu can totally monopolise a man's conduct and social integration, so can caste, when strictly adhered to – directing how he carries out his toilet, eats, dresses, gets up in the morning and goes to sleep at night, walks down a street, pays a visit, goes on a journey, makes conversation, prays, works, celebrates a festival or ceremonies concerning death, burial and cremation, and even sits down. Another similarity between Hinduism and caste is the attention to ritual – the different ways in which one cooks, when one washes, whom one can engage in conversation and how one drapes one's sari or dhoti is traditionally solely attributed to one's caste.

The practice of caste varies tremendously with area, and within specific regions is more closely associated with jati, or subcaste.

In any district there will not be just four castes, but hundreds of endogamous subcastes. Despite Hindus being the majority in India, each caste Hindu believes himself to be in a minority, so strongly does he feel himself to be a part of his own subcaste. Indeed it is the division between families which gives village life in Hindu society much of its character, the design of this fragmentation providing the structure of daily life and human contact. Few women, apart from midwives and teachers, have contact with others outside their own caste.

At the outset, subcastes emerged through migration, but change of occupation was later responsible for the formation of new subcastes. The whole of the system assured subsistence to one another, thousands of communities broken into small units orientated towards the needs of the whole.

Although the function of caste in a village cannot be generalised – every small village is its own self-sufficient 'little republic' – at its simplest each jati member behaves in a similar way to his forefathers. All actions and deeds are worked out for him: when he starts his apprenticeship with his father in the family trade, when he marries and all the daily rituals of eating and cleaning. He takes water from the well of the grandson of the man from whom his grandfather took water. If his father drank fermented drinks, so does he. If he is twice-born, he may wash his feet before eating, as his father did. Remarriage of widows still is rarely permissible for the higher castes, causing great hardship for a young bride if her husband dies before she has produced children. As long as the line is toed, order is maintained and undoubtedly devotion to one job brings about a high standard of craftsmanship in the artisans' skills.

Funeral rites are determined by caste rules. Only twice-born Hindus cremate rather than bury their dead. Economics may have initially dictated this practice, the wood for a funeral pyre being so costly. When there is a religious ceremony involving the whole village, who is responsible for what job follows the same pattern as for previous generations. Who constructs the deities, who sweeps around the temple, who sweeps inside the temple, which family of Brahmins bathes and dresses the deity, who carries the deity in the procession, who plays in the village band, who is permitted to approach the deity and give offerings of food at specified times –

there is a part, a particular role to be played by all the community, by the barber, the carpenter, the sweeper, everyone.

At grassroots level, village politics are governed by the caste council, more commonly known as the panchayat. Should a man have to give evidence before the panchayat, he is often asked to take an oath, similar to that in English Law when a witness is required to lay his hands on the *Holy Bible*. There are various methods of doing this – sometimes the witness has to hold a vessel containing water from the Ganges or touch the holy sweet basil plant. Some communities have the practice comic to Western eyes of making someone swear while holding on to the tail of a cow. The most common punishment meted out for caste misbehaviour is excommunication and all retributions are intended to make the culprit feel humiliated.

Caste councils today are responsible for the overall continuing strength of the system, making it well nigh impossible to air a grievance over discrimination and receive one's just rights in the eyes of the law. However, when immigration to the city takes place, rigid caste practice, except the rules concerning marriage, gradually breaks down due to the effort of joining in the tumultuous rat race for daily survival.

The lowest group in today's society, the outcastes or Untouchables (also referred to as the scheduled castes) were originally tribal groups conquered by the higher castes who, by dint of birth, were considered unworthy of inclusion in the system. To bestow some dignity and encouragement to the most disadvantaged, Mahatma Gandhi renamed the Untouchables as Harijans (children of God) and set an example by requiring everyone to take a turn at cleaning the latrines (one of the allotted tasks of the Untouchables) in the ashram over which he presided. However, today many Harijans still clean the streets and latrines, and deal with the flesh of dead animals, which includes all leatherwork and shoemaking and beating the drum at village functions, weddings and funerals. They also work on the land, frequently in a situation of bonded labour. The Chamars, the traditional dealers in dead cattle, have a higher status in village life than the Doms, known in some areas as the Bhangis, the sweepers and removers of sewage, although both groups are Untouchables. Harsh attitudes to an Untouchable are simply explained in that it is believed that he owes his pitiful existence to a personal misdeed in his former life. If he accepts his station in life and performs his duty conscientiously, then he will be rewarded with a better station in the next life, or better still no rebirth at all. But the Untouchables are not outside the caste system altogether. Their role has been important in maintaining Hindu daily life. All their allotted tasks have been necessary to propagate the continuation of the system. They have been essential in preserving the 'ritual' purity of the Brahminic groups, and by performing various 'polluting' tasks for the other groups have ensured the interdependence between them all. The term 'Untouchable' today encompasses those who are deprived of political and economic power and Untouchability cannot be overcome until the notion of the purity of Brahmins has been eradicated.

'Desecration' offers perhaps the most apt analogy of 'pollution'. On a journey through India, one's senses can be continually reviled by the lack of general hygiene – children urinating in the gutters, men defecating along the roadside, piles of discarded rubbish dumped in public places – and the notion of anyone remaining unsullied in such surroundings seems ridiculous. In Patna, where the Ganges flows full and wide, one can observe a man sifting through the charred remains of his father, rinsing the pot of ashes in the murky water, while, alongside, a dhobi will be washing a pile of white dhotis and cotton saris. However, the Ganges is the holiest of rivers, and whatever diseased remains have been dumped there its water is always considered pure and cleansing.

All forms of menstrual blood are polluting. Traditionally a menstruating woman totally separated herself from the family, her food being left for her on a veranda. The dhobi who washed the blood-stained clothes was an Untouchable.

In preparation, vegetarian food is less susceptible to the risks of pollution and most Brahmins are vegetarians. Milk, ghee and yoghurt are still regarded as cleansing agents and from the Vedic age the cow has been venerated as the cosmic symbol of the universal mother and source of pure food. Eating in India is not associated, as in the West, with a chance to make pleasant conversation. Although the food itself often tastes delicious, for most it is a technical operation. Many Brahmins eat quietly and alone in a corner of their home, having first observed numerous rituals of purification. Indian hospitality is legend but on many occasions I have been brought dish after dish of delicious curries and had to eat alone while an entire family watched me. As I have urged my hosts to partake of the food with me, they have shaken their heads. They would eat when I have departed, maybe even ceremoniously wiping over where I have washed my face and rinsed my hands. Brahmins usually treat cooking with the utmost care, each preparation a religious ceremony in itself, even though the staple diet is simply boiled rice or chapattis (pancakes of unleavened flour mixed with water and cooked on an iron griddle).

Should a person of an inferior caste touch the earthen water pot of a Brahmin, the pot may then have to be destroyed. However, water from the Ganges can be brought to the home of a Brahmin by an Untouchable, its purity and sanctity being unsulliable. The influence of Islam and the emergence of Sikhism have greatly weakened the notion of Untouchability in northern India, and for generations Hindus living in Delhi have paid Muslim porters to bring water to their homes, where it is not uncommon for twice-born gentlemen to share a pipe, such practice in the south provoking horror at the risk of passing on saliva. I was once amused to see a group sharing a pipe, each individual inhaling the smoke through a thin muslin cloth.

Many Brahmins still avoid physical contact with members of the following subcastes: Dhobis, because they wash the clothes of menstruating women; Chamars, because they work with cow hide; Doms, because they are responsible for disposing of the corpses of dead animals; and Sweepers, because they clean latrines.

Some traditional Brahmins will not use public transport, because they are unable to avoid contact with a polluting agent. For the same reason, large temples are often filled only with female worshippers, who are less worried about taboos of pollution and more concerned with their devotion and praying for their families' spiritual growth.

Should a well become polluted through being used by an Untouchable or through a dog accidentally drowning in the water, purification can easily be arranged by pouring into it either a bucketful of Ganges water or drops of cow's urine from a small brass vessel – a strange notion considering the germs contained by both. In desert areas where Untouchables have asserted their rights by insisting on drawing water from the communal well, Brahmins have been known to send a camel to fetch water from a well some miles away, to avoid polluting themselves.

No one seems sure why overseas travel is prohibited to strict Hindus but the most likely explanation is because observation of caste rules was impractical or even impossible away from home and the only way a family could prevent themselves from being polluted by their travelling member would be to excommunicate him on his return. One of the most efficacious means of purification is to drink a mixture of the five products of the cow, a paste of milk, clarified butter, curds and urine bound together with a little dung. Many a hapless member of a traditional Brahmin family has returned from three years of studying law or commerce in a European university and consumed a mouthful of this vile mixture before being allowed to embrace his own parents.

In the larger cities today, where space and accommodation are extremely limited, the notion of pollution becomes absurd. When caste conscious village folk come to the town in search of a job, taboos of pollution are the first to be broken if they are fortunate in finding work. In a village everyone knows everyone else's caste, whereas in a city nobody would bother to find out unless they were to be invited into someone's home. Intermingling in the temple becomes inevitable and public transport, too, throws people together into close contact, and the need to make a journey far exceeds most people's desire to keep themselves unpolluted. People have begun to accept behaviour outside their homes which they would not tolerate within. Many businessmen will eat meat curries and drink alcoholic beverages in a five-star hotel with a foreign client, particularly if a beneficial deal is about to be made, whereas in their own home they take off their shoes on the threshold, are strict vegetarians, their wives eat at a separate table during their monthly periods and sweepers are only allowed to clean the toilet if there is another servant to wipe over where they have walked. Even the most lowly clerk will live a life of double standards – he will ignore all caste taboos in the office, yet on reaching home take off his Western-style clothes, have a ceremonial shower and put on his traditional kurta pyjama outfit, thus reintegrating himself in his own caste.

Since India secured Independence from the British in 1947, political leaders and thinkers have generally acknowledged that the caste system is an aberration and should be abolished. Prime Minister Nehru made caste discrimination illegal, believing not only that its continuation was a hindrance to industrial development and economic advance but also that the repression it imposed on those outside the system was discreditable in a modern humanitarian society. Mahatma Gandhi more realistically observed that no civil law could break down overnight a system which had governed the people's minds for over three thousand years. Moreover, he appreciated the benefits of caste in a society as complex as India's where each group of efficient and skilled artisans performed an appointed task, but he condemned the notion of marriage taking place strictly within one's clan, perceiving a continuing injustice where a person's value was simply attached to the situation of birth.

In fact the basic right in India that all are equal in the eyes of the law was established at the beginning of the British Rule in India over a hundred years ago. However, one hallmark of the British Empire was never to interfere in the religious and cultural behaviour of its subjects. Caste was regarded by the English as an offspring of Hinduism so they never meddled with the workings of the system, their responsibility to the Crown being simply to maintain civil order and encourage economic growth.

Human injustice exists in every country in the world, but in India it is aggravated by the caste system – inequality exists here in perhaps its most complex and bizarre form, the social order being so strongly formalised. In rural areas, from cradle to grave, men and women cannot break away from their social environment however hard they strive. The continuing strength of caste continually amazes every foreigner who travels through the country, although at its most conventional it is certainly on the decline.

Caste is a peculiarly Indian phenomenon, although there are traits similar to it in other societies, the British class system for one, but in its fullest sense nothing is comparable, and as Hindus have emigrated overseas, to Sri Lanka, Bali, African countries and West Indies, so too has the system spread. It has proved to be historically very stable (not that this is a reason for its continuation to be advocated), and its existence has provided a unity that no other political formula could have ensured for a nation of such diversity.

Indeed, paradoxically, the Mughal conquests fortified the caste system. The natural indigenous leaders, the princely Rajputs, were overpowered, and the powers of the priests, the Brahmins, were thus strengthened. The system continued to be upheld through the intervention of Islam because the rigidity of intermarrying within social groups maintained a distance for the Hindus from their invaders. For a Hindu to marry a Muslim meant immediate excommunication from his extended family group. Yet it is interesting to see how caste practice has penetrated the Muslim communities, people for whom concepts of rebirth and preordained destiny are foreign – a form of social harmony evolved as certain aspects of Hindu behaviour organically crept in, more in the form of guilds than the adoption of concepts of pollution. And in their turn Hindus too have adopted some Muslim habits, notably women taking on purdah.

Another way in which caste has filtered across to other religions has been through the conversion of Hindus to Islam, Christianity, Buddhism and Sikhism. A direct revolt against caste, this offered the quickest escape from the horrors of Untouchability. However, caste never invaded the British way of thinking, most probably because the majority of the British, where they could afford to, continued to send their children back to England for their education and many of them, even if they were eventually unable to afford the passage, would plan to return to England once they had reached retirement age.

The adoption of Islam and Christianity by the lower castes has often presented a challenge to the domination and power of the landlords. Although this is the desired effect, it is still noticeable how both Muslims and Christians have failed profoundly to alter their economic status and how their communities are, in rural areas, subjected to living outside the domain of the higher castes.

To break away from one's caste usually causes trauma as it so often means breaking from one's own family and group, and such ostracisation can only be beneficial when a person has the strength, outstanding courage or means to make a purposeful life quite away from the comfort of his society.

However, there are many devout Hindus who fervently want to pull down the barriers, and one finds now that strict adherence to the old social mores are becoming more relaxed, especially the restrictions regarding eating habits amongst the lower castes. People often accept an invitation to visit another's home although many will bring their own tiffin cans with food prepared in their own kitchen. The changes and shift in economic power, as were experienced during the Industrial Revolution in Europe during the last century, mean that the ritually superior group no longer continues to enjoy economic superiority, and it is not unusual now to find a Brahmin living in penury.

Education and the introduction of radio and television are breaking down the old taboos. If the head of the panchayat hires a television and can charge the villagers 50 paise, say, to watch the Sunday afternoon film, he is hardly likely to forgo the chance to make as much money as possible by insisting that the castes be segregated. Yet, sadly, the attitude that continues to remain most strong is the emphatic belief among upper castes that they are a superior species to the lower echelons of society. Even today, despite the legislation condemning caste practice, Untouchables continue to suffer appalling indignities. There is still probably not one village in the whole of India where the Harijans will use the same well as the upper castes. Location of dwellings may partly explain this, but inherently no Harijan will seek out trouble from a caste Hindu, so dependent is he economically on his patronage. Land reforms have not allowed more than a few acres to pass into the hands of the Harijans, so they are still reliant on the landlords for work. In a country with virtually none of the social security benefits enjoyed in the West, land is man's most important possession and the only real form of recognised wealth.

In the villages today a high percentage still follow their caste professions, namely sweepers, goldsmiths, confectioners, barbers, dhobis, potters and weavers. On the artisan level one rarely encounters a caste Hindu undertaking a profession which would lower his status, although for decades Brahmins, after academic education, have joined the medical profession, and have usually been excommunicated in the process because of their association with the highly polluting practice of childbirth. However, the introduction of electricity and engineering facilities is gradually breaking down the artisan's commitment to his own skill. As some professions become redundant, people from a variety of castes are compelled to apply for industrial work, simply to feed their families. Economic need, rather than laws passed in New Delhi, is breaking down caste.

A close inspection of urban bourgeois Indian society reveals a complex entanglement of languages and castes, politics and power. The underprivileged groups are now beginning to receive more information of the possibilities of change outside their small units with which to build upon their feeling of indignation at their lot, and enlightened educated Hindus are at pains to find means of abolishing the system.

Technology and science have encouraged all sections of society to aspire to material rather than emotional wealth. Lower castes desiring to climb the social ladder regard the step to be economic rather than spiritual. Sadly, I have noticed how financial success is the goal and to achieve this people will sacrifice the chance of educating their children and even forgo a decent diet if it means that they can own a television set, a symbol of prestige and honour. People are caught up in the cloying cobweb of videos and radios, a tragic onslaught in a country where for centuries people have devoted their thoughts to the study of what is the meaning of life. This desire to emulate our Western behaviour is eroding what is special about Indian culture.

Moreover, useful social and economic progress has been hindered by the belief that misfortune must be endured without complaint and come to terms with, rather than the root causes of inequality and injustice tackled. This belief acts as a form of control over a massive population, in that they passively accept that much of their miserable condition is simply the will of God and often adopt an attitude of tolerance towards a wretched existence, but it also creates frustrations for philanthropic individuals attempting to introduce reforms in health care, education and family planning.

In the northern Hindi-speaking states such as Bihar, Uttar Pradesh and Haryana, where there is still great backwardness in rural life, general prevailing poverty and very little upward social mobility, the caste system is at its most strong, the people firmly entrenched in its laws and customs. At election time, it is not political ideology but the caste factor which matters. The political parties field candidates either from the majority caste living in a particular area, or, where there is greater dependence on landowners, from the landowning caste who will control the votes of their agricultural employees. Most candidates who emerge from the lower castes full of energy and idealism rapidly lose track of their initial goals and are sidetracked and swayed by the inescapable corruption of power politics. It is being in power which counts, not the principles one holds. Socialists believe that there will be no true democracy while elections are held on the caste line. Democratic socialism and caste are diametrically opposed phenomena because caste practice spells gross oppression of the backward classes, scheduled castes and tribes who, combined, constitute the majority. The dominant section of the government is from the upper orders – rich people who often employ dacoits to capture polling booths in depressed areas and sway the vote in their direction. In these instances, fear of harassment, the practical impossibility of being able to lodge a complaint with a police force which has probably been bribed anyway, and the sheer logistics of transport and telecommunication in many villages, usually means that the lower orders accept their lot in resigned silence. The daily personal struggle for survival is more important than representation in government in the capital.

Liberal, well-heeled inhabitants of Delhi and Bombay drawing rooms may nod their heads wisely: 'There is no caste system in India today. This is a thing of the past.' They fail to notice that nearly every day the leading newspapers report violent incidents and death triggered by caste grievances. For nearly three years, there have been daily stories of agitation in the western state of Gujurat. Caste Hindus have been protesting against the government's reservationist policies which hold posts and places in the universities especially for the backward classes and scheduled castes in an attempt to encourage equality. Thousands of lives have been lost, homes burnt to the ground, shops looted and livelihoods destroyed, and, despite the imposition of numerous curfews and stringent legal action, the disturbances still continue. Yet, surprisingly, the provocation for much of the trouble is from the intensely conservative and orthodox

11 An elderly ropemaker   12 A potter in Udaipur   13 A shepherd takes a nap while his young son minds the flock   14 Three generations of a Harijan family work together in the paddy fields

sections of society, the middle classes and upper castes, status rather than economic deprivation being their motive.

In recent years in Bihar, notorious for its rigid practice of caste discrimination, two notable and vicious massacres attracted wide coverage in the international press. The late Indira Gandhi, during her years in opposition, rode 16 miles on an elephant through flood-stricken countryside to Belchi to offer her sympathy to the bereaved relatives of a community of Harijans who were killed and maimed following a battle with upper-caste oppressors, and in Pipra Harijans were roasted alive when their homes were set alight by agitators.

Stories of caste carnage are so common that they cease to have impact, although the details are indeed horrendous and shocking. The extent of brutality can be awesome, and it is so often provoked by relatively minor incidents. During one of my stays in India I was horrified to read about a caste group of agriculturalists known as the Yadavs who resented the purchase of a few acres of fertile land from an old Rajput by the Binds, a weaker rival caste. During one November night, prior to Diwali celebrations, the Yadavs poured petrol on the huts of the sleeping Binds and set them on fire. As the petrified inhabitants attempted to flee, choking and blinded by the thick smoke, they ran towards their attackers, who shot or hacked the men to death. Then the women were rounded up and systematically stripped and raped. Over a hundred people lost their lives and, although police enquiries were instigated, the truth was submerged, and the local magistrate, who was led to believe that only five men died in a skirmish provoked by a small domestic argument, said there wasn't enough evidence to prosecute those who were culpable.

There is a moving story of an enlightened Brahmin government employee from Patna. While studying in the local university, he became aware of the unfair advantage he had over his college mates and, seeing the evil of untouchability to be still a part of the Indian social system and the caste barrier yet to be broken, he married a Harijan girl from the Madhubani district of Bihar. While in local employment, the circumstances of his marriage were tolerated, but on promotion he took his wife and three young children to the city where he was mercilessly hounded by caste Hindu colleagues. His wife was refused

15 A village shepherd at election time poses in front of campaign graffiti

medical treatment when she was badly burnt, his life threatened unless he obtained a divorce and finally he was handed his notice without a reason being given, except that he was considered unsuitable. The case received considerable attention in New Delhi, but has now been relegated to a large file marked 'Pending'. Meanwhile the family have returned to his village, ostracised, penniless and without work, their survival being dependent on the goodwill of the wife's father.

On a prosperous eastern tobacco plantation in Andhra Pradesh, central India, five Harijans were hacked to death after a Harijan youth apparently watered his buffalo at the communal reservoir letting some of the water slip back into the well, thereby unleashing a massive backlog of tension between the landlords and peasants.

Sadly, the token gestures originally introduced to break down the caste system have backfired by both endorsing and promoting its existence, and at present anti-caste legislation is increasing caste tension. It is one thing to introduce new laws but quite another to ensure that these laws are observed. In a country as large as India, few will fight for their rights if it means risking the chance of feeding their families.

But how else to reverse a code of behaviour which has governed the lives of a whole population for over three thousand years? In the forty years since Independence was gained, leadership has been almost continuously in the hands of those with Western thoughts and education, men who have endeavoured to dissipate ancient concepts, but at grassroots level social change is acutely slow.

4

A Marwari Family in Bombay

As the plane approaches the runway at Santa Cruz airport one cannot fail to be stirred by the dreadful sight below of the cardboard and tin shacks where thousands make their home. Yet, every time I go to Bombay, on the taxi ride into the city my visual and emotional senses are excited and stirred. It is a huge port and the industrial capital of India, an extraordinary metropolis throbbing with a rhythm of life that absorbs many millions of people of scores of different castes, creeds and cultures.

On my first visit, many years ago, I spent an afternoon wandering around the antique curio and silver bazaars and that evening rode on the pillion of a small scooter while my host threaded the vehicle through the narrow lanes where prostitutes and merchants live side by side. It was Diwali, the Hindu New Year, and the carved wooden balconies were all strung with coloured lanterns, the dark houses filled with the light of flickering candles. Beggars slept on the pavements and young women's giggles could be heard from behind closed shutters, joy and despair intermingled. On subsequent visits I photographed mobile crèches set up by voluntary agencies to help young mothers, barely out of puberty, who sift and carry sand and cement on building construction sites for ten hours a day. I visited orphanages where children, often found abandoned in the streets, are cared for while suitable homes are found in the West.

Paradoxically, in the evenings I sat on the veranda of my host's spacious apartment and was served gin and tonic with ice and a slice of lime. I watched the evening shadows fall, listening to the sounds of the ocean, a gentle sea breeze blowing through the tall coconut palms which fringe the shore. The climate here is perhaps the most agreeable in the whole of India – it is never too hot, nor too cold, and with unfailing regularity the monsoon rains come in early June every year.

I wanted to talk to a city-dwelling family who were very wealthy and in Bombay such a family is not hard to find. Many of the city's financial ventures are controlled by the community of Parsis, Persian migrants who came here over a thousand years ago. One of its most powerful members is the Tata family, renowned industrialists, whose might and strength is matched only by the Hindu Birla family. The Birlas are Marwaris – a large community from the Vayshya caste whose aggressive business acumen is well known in all major cities in India. There are many Marwari families living and working in Bombay but, understandably, when I spoke to them most were wary of my curiosity and prying, accustomed to the ruthlessness of journalists. It took much persuasion for a family to take me into their confidence and, in part, I feel I have betrayed them. I have endeavoured to be fair and impartial but found it impossible not to make a few unkind judgments when I perceived great wealth being openly squandered in a city where so many people go hungry.

I met Mr and Mrs Gordhondas at a wedding party (in industrial cities the English form of address prevails), and it was they who approached me first. I told them quite openly the nature of my research and Ranjit Gordhondas gave me his business card. Out of his wife's earshot he suggested we meet for lunch one day, then in front of her, seemingly to enlist her approval of his being friendly with me, he told me that their daughter Shalini was soon to be married so maybe this would be an opportunity to witness a marriage from the outset. They concurred that I would be welcome to spend as much time with them in their home as I wanted.

I paid my first visit the following Sunday morning. Shalini was getting dressed for her engagement party and there was much excitement as she was to wear a sari for the first time. She was only sixteen years old and her sister-in-law, Rithu, was in charge. I went into the bedroom and sat down on the bed with my notebook.

'Don't pick it up like that. You'll crush the material and it will look terrible,' scolded Rithu, as she deftly pleated the folds of gorgeous silk.

A sumptuous buffet luncheon was to be held at the Centaur Hotel, a five-star complex situated close to the International Airport – a venue selected, they explained, so that the prospective groom's father could return home immediately after the ceremony to resume a hectic business schedule.

Rithu began to make up the young girl's eyes. Then she picked up a tube of bright red lipstick. Shalini started to protest. She had never worn make-up on her face.

'Look, sit still. You've got to highlight your features otherwise nothing will show up on the video film or the photographs.'

I later found out that Shalini was still attending the Roman Catholic Fort convent school in the centre of the city, there being an element of snobbery for a Hindu to be educated by Christian nuns. She was preparing for her tenth grade examinations, equivalent to the English GCSEs. If successful she hoped to study for a further two years. She was more bewildered than indignant at the notion of her forthcoming wedding, but her future parents-in-law had assured her parents that they were quite happy for her to complete her studies after her marriage. When her father first suggested the union Shalini was, not surprisingly, a little afraid. Rithu was against the whole idea.

'I told her not to let him do this to her. She's so young and could have such a wonderful time if she went to college, enjoying herself, with no family problems to worry about. She doesn't want to get herself bogged down looking after a husband, but I think they blackmailed her.'

Shalini's mother had recently been suffering from high blood pressure. The family doctor suggested that this could be due to anxiety brought on through worrying about a suitable match for her daughter. Now her husband had made a good deal with a wealthy Marwari family from Madras, so she should be happy and her blood pressure soon would come down. Thus Shalini was persuaded.

Marriage for the Marwaris is the most important alliance of their lifetime. Often they engage an astrologer to read a child's horoscope at birth, to establish favourable conditions. Then, in order to save time and money, sometimes before the child is in its teens, they circulate a copy of the astrological chart among suitable contenders for the child's hand. In order to find a good husband, Shalini's father had employed a broker from a firm who specialised in transactions of this nature. Their charge was fixed in accordance with the circumstances of the groom's family. They presented a variety of young men and then checked out the financial standing and credibility of the families of those considered suitable.

'I insisted absolutely that my daughter should marry a young man from Madras, Calcutta or Delhi. In all these cities there are fine communities of Marwaris. It wouldn't be good for her to stay in Bombay because whenever there's a small problem she will think she can run home to her mother. Unlike her brothers she has to be quite independent from us, make a complete break and start a new life with her new family; remaining in this city would be bad for her future domestic harmony. I've been chided for marrying her off before she has completed her studies but I believe absolutely that she should be settled into marriage early on, otherwise, like my stupid, restless daughter-in-law Rithu, she may get some silly ideas into her head.' As he spoke of his daughter there was little hint of paternal affection.

A husband had been found, a young man of twenty-two years, Jayanti Kumar. He worked with his father in Madras, manufacturing jute sacks with a sideline in synthetic fibres and computers. They were also exploring the possibilities of expanding their business into other forms of packing. Mr Gordhondas's large range of business interests in textiles excited their curiosity. Perhaps after the wedding the two families could merge some of their business interests.

A month earlier Jayanti had come to Bombay to meet Shalini. His maternal uncle had brought him to the Gordhondases' apartment one afternoon. In the presence of the uncle and Mrs Gordhondas they had silently scrutinised each other over cups of tea. The introduction had been so that both parties were given an opportunity to reject the union, but since childhood they had been conditioned to accept their parents' choice. Aware that for them marriage came first and familiarity later, they did not seek an instant rapport, rather a reassurance that they were not revolted by the prospect of spending the rest of their lives together. The conversation was kept to generalities and after a meeting of less than one hour they agreed to proceed with the union. In the preceding weeks Jayanti had twice made contact with Shalini over the telephone.

'We didn't discuss anything personal. I just told him about my studies but the line was very poor and I don't think he heard much but he did say that if I fail my exams I can go to the high school in Madras.'

However, despite his agreement, it seemed unlikely she would continue her education. When a dowry is enticing, prospective parents-in-law often make such promises and when the marriage has taken place they change their minds. Shalini's parents made enquiries into Jayanti's financial prospects but had little knowledge of the domestic arrangements in Madras. Jayanti's parents wanted to proceed immediately with the wedding before the onset of the rainy season but Mr Gordhondas persuaded them to allow his daughter to complete the current academic year. After the engagement party she would be swotting up on history, political science and economics. Meanwhile her mother would send to Madras weekly air-freight parcels of sweets, silks and fruits, gifts to signify her delight and approval of the engagement.

At last, her silk brocade sari correctly adjusted and the loose end draped over her head in a mark of respect, Shalini joined her family, and they were whisked in a fleet of hired Ambassador cars to the Centaur Hotel. Only a dozen or so relatives of the groom were present but the occasion was attended by nearly a hundred relatives and Marwari acquaintances of Mr and Mrs Gordhondas. The arrival of Shalini and her party at the Coromandel Suite fortunately coincided with that of Jayanti and his family. He and his future bride greeted each other nervously and the other guests followed suit. The younger guests bent down and touched their elders' feet, a traditional form of greeting to show respect. As soon as everyone was assembled, Shalini and Jayanti were seated side by side for a ceremony of introduction. Jayanti's grandmother gave Shalini gifts of gold jewellery, three large bracelets embossed with rubies, two long pendants and a pair of ear-rings moulded in the shape of elephants and studded with rubies. Then Mr Gordhondas placed in the old lady's hand a small black leather pouch containing a deposit on the dowry, a prearranged sum of 8 lakh rupees, around £40,000. Jayanti's father sighed with relief and the rest of his family smiled. After a photograph session everyone proceeded to the dining table which was laden with large silver plates heaped with mounds of spiced and creamy vegetables.

The Marwaris are a community that originally emerged from the Vayshya Caste. As the princely Rajputs gained political strength in Rajasthan two centuries ago, they formed a mutually beneficial bond with a local group of merchants living in Marwar, a small town some 50 miles south-east of Jodhpur. These merchants had taken advantage of the trade routes which had evolved between China and North Africa, Europe and the wealthier Arab countries such as Persia. To the large caravans of traders who passed through bearing silks, spices, coffee and other exotic goods they contributed their own home produce, sugar, opium, shawls and a greater variety of spices. As they expanded their clan roots strengthened and an alliance with the warrior-like Rajputs ensued. The Rajputs ensured territorial stability while the Marwaris gave their ruling lords financial backing. As these merchant communities grew in number in the course of time, their experience and familiarity in business led to many of them becoming money lenders. They also built lavish havelis for themselves – large mansions surrounded by enclosed courtyards where they shut away their wives and children in strict seclusion.

In the nineteenth century, during the early days of the British Raj, the busy overland trading routes and caravan serais were gradually superseded by the new railway system and by sea routes via the larger ports. Many Marwari communities, with customary commercial astuteness, seized upon the new trading opportunities and migrated eastward to Bihar and Assam to expand their trade into jute, wool and cotton. As travel became easier the more successful families filtered towards the other large cities of India – Calcutta, Delhi, Hyderabad, Madras and Bombay. Although the community is now scattered throughout the whole country the Marwaris still maintain a strong link with their ancestral homeland, in the same way as

Jews in Europe and the United States consider Israel to be their cultural home. Wide business interests led to political interests and many Marwaris played an important role in the formation and early organisation of the Congress party.

Marwaris have acquired, through the years, a very unpopular image for themselves. During the Raj, Indians believed that the British were the most efficient businessmen in the world after the Jews. Yet, where making money was concerned, I have heard it said that one Marwari is equal to ten Jews. Today Marwaris have a reputation of being incurable workaholics, thinking only of accumulating more and more money by toiling morning, noon and night. Everything on which they spend money is bought to increase their status, so that they are seen to have the latest gadgets, clothes, jewellery, paintings or sculpture. They are a very close community, socialising almost exclusively among their own kind. If someone does break away he runs the risk of being completely ostracised and he is unlikely to find someone from another community to help him should he wish to start a new venture. However, although they are secretive by nature, once their confidence and trust is gained they will back a friend to the hilt.

In the past, Marwaris sought out as many monopolies in as many trades as they could muster. Hindus are generally uncompetitive and easy-going but after the decline of the British Raj the Marwaris rapidly gained control of much of industry in the new state of India. In some cities the Marwaris are more powerful than most prominent politicians and it often appears that they have complete financial control over all shopkeepers and traders. Their habits, too, are very different from most Hindus, who take care with their personal cleanliness – they generally use very little water, even for drinking, therefore hygiene is a low priority. This is attributable to their origins in Rajasthan where water was a precious commodity preserved for quenching thirst and watering the camels. They used sand to scour out their cooking pots and never used water to clean themselves or their utensils. Over the generations the habit of not using water has continued; they now give their children sweet aerated drinks rather than plain water.

Fifty-five-year-old Ranjit Gordhondas came to Bombay from Calcutta with his uncle some thirty-five years earlier. His father had died when he was a young boy, and as soon as he had completed his studies he was deemed a suitable candidate to be trained to oversee the family's expansion of business interests. Five years later, after he had grasped the rudiments of trade and finance, his arranged marriage to Kamala took place. Kamala was only fifteen years old. In her own words, she was still a child, totally unprepared and uninformed of the realities of married life. Within three years she had two sons, Ashish and Santanu. To both her and her husband's surprise their daughter Shalini was born nearly ten years after Santanu. Kamala is now in her mid-forties. She has a sallow complexion and her features hint at some mixed ancestry from the north-east of the country, towards the Tibetan border. Her two sons are now married and both still live at home with their young wives.

Kamala Gordhondas confided in me that being a mother to sons has been one of the most profound pleasures for her, although she is concerned about the future welfare of her first-born. Intelligent, introverted and hardworking, Ashish has chosen a career rarely pursued by a Marwari. His keen interest in scientific subjects at school led him to study medicine. During the early years of his medical training he met and fell in love with Rithu, the daughter of one of his professors. His parents pleaded with him to relinquish her but finally relented. Kamala was secretly proud of him for choosing so noble a profession, and wishing only for his happiness welcomed Rithu into their home, accepting her as a daughter. Kamala sees in Ashish characteristics reminiscent of her own father. At the outset his wish to be a doctor and specialise in paediatrics was fuelled by a philanthropic desire to help the weaker sections of society. However, frustrated by impossible working conditions and a general lack of facilities in the public sector, he was now hoping to set up his own private practice. Determined to reach the top of his profession, he took an early breakfast before leaving for the day's attendance at the hospital, and then went straight to the university library and spent all the evening hours studying for further examinations. He rarely came home before midnight.

But Rithu had found it difficult to come to terms with both Ashish's obsessiveness with work and the traditional ways of his family. Her own family belonged to a Brahmin subcaste.

'When some of my forefathers started to practise medicine at the beginning of this century, they became outcaste because they handled dead bodies. They were forbidden to take wives from Brahmin families so started to marry into the Kshatrya castes, and their children formed a subcaste called Baydyas. So technically speaking I'm a higher caste than the Gordhondases. But caste is of no significance to either me or my family, although they were very concerned at first when I fell in love with a Marwari. My upbringing was very easy-going. I think perhaps that was why Ashish liked me so much. When we first met he would come and spend the weekends with us at our apartment and I think he just found us very undemanding and relaxed. I don't know what has changed since, why he can't stop working all the time, but I'm thinking of doing some secretarial training so perhaps I can help him when he does set up his own practice.'

In fact, although he had been unable to say as much to his wife, Ashish cherished a desire to make himself quite independent from his father and to make a separate life for his wife and the children he hoped to have. He knew this was quite impossible as long as he was financially dependent.

The personality of Ashish's younger brother, Santanu, was completely different although he had inherited the same attitude to hard work. He was both sociable and gregarious. He was the proud owner of a splendid silver-brown Mercedes-Benz he had bought from a friend in Delhi, but would not reveal how much he paid for it, not wanting the taxman at his throat! Foreign cars were subject to very heavy import duties and considered not only a luxury but also something of a status symbol.

'I am completing my studies in accountancy and working with my father at present but I may not stay in textiles. I am always on the lookout for anything financially enticing, such as household cleaners, manufacturing of tools and spare parts, or commodities. I have a good friend who processes synthetic waste into fibre which is then used for stuffing toys and quilts and for making wadding for special packaging. In three years his turnover has trebled and I can see that the key to his success has been shrewd marketing and doing nothing whatsoever for charity.'

Eighteen months earlier Santanu had married Premula, a Marwari girl from Delhi. It was an arranged marriage and his mother was optimistic about it. After an opulent wedding at Premula's home they went to the beach resort of Goa for their honeymoon. They were quite taken aback by the foreigners sunbathing naked although they adopted a mixture of curiosity and tolerance towards them on the beach. However, when the same people approached them in the hotel restaurant, Santanu, not wanting close physical contact, would immediately lead his young bride to another table.

Like Rithu, Premula was already suffering from long hours spent on her own. At first she got on well with her new family. Her mother-in-law seemed a kind woman, eager to make her feel at home, introducing her to their relatives and showing her the shops. But after a few months she began to notice how her leisure time seemed to be manipulated by Kamala so that she spent little time socially with Santanu. Every evening Kamala came into their bedroom, sat on their bed and waited until her son returned home. When he came in she talked to him as though Premula wasn't even there.

'I know she is in fact very lonely herself as her own husband is rarely there but I find it extremely hard to accept how possessive she is of her sons. Sometimes she even falls asleep on our bed. I'm always asking Santanu to talk to her but he gets angry with me and says he doesn't want to hurt her feelings. But I think he really enjoys being cosseted by her. He's always been given as much money as he wanted and all other kinds of luxuries. He doesn't want to give any of them up.'

Keen and conditioned to make a go of her marriage, Premula often accompanied Santanu on business trips to Lucknow and Kanpur, but there was little to occupy her during the day. She watched video films in the hotel bedroom and telephoned her childhood friends. She confessed to being extremely bored for much of the time but knew that the situation would change when she started her own family. Unfortunately she and Rithu, although tolerant of each other, had not become close. Yet Premula did enjoy life in Bombay. During the day she went shopping in the Crawford Market, a large colourful arcade full of fruit and vegetable stalls, visited coffee shops, and attended cooking lessons and classes in sewing and embroidery. In the evening she often strolled along the sea front with her mother-in-law. Once a week a young man came to the family's apartment to give manicures and pedicures to all the ladies.

Both sons would continue living with their parents for some time to come. Quite apart from the exorbitant price of real estate in Bombay, a Marwari son rarely chooses to leave home during the first years of married life unless he moves his business interests to another city. Great importance is attached to public shows of family unity on collective weekend outings to five-star hotels or the Bombay Cricket Club.

Kamala Gordhondas's feelings for her daughter were more ambiguous. Knowing that when her daughter married and left the family home her contact with her would be minimal, Kamala began distancing herself emotionally from Shalini early on, preferring to concentrate on teaching the young girl how to become a good wife.

The Gordhondas family lived in a large apartment block overlooking Marine Drive, a handsome palm-fringed boulevard which sweeps and curves around Back Bay, facing west towards the Arabian Sea. On the promenade young boys rollerskated and tourists rode in old wooden carriages pulled by emaciated horses. A coconut vendor and a seller of belpuri, a snack of cereal mixed with spices, plied their wares. To the north, beyond the legendary Chowpatty beach, lies Malabar Hill, a leafy enclave where Bombay's film stars have their homes. To the south, massive high-rise apartments are clustered together on land recently reclaimed from the sea.

The Gordhondases' second-floor flat was situated at the rear of a block overlooking the Bombay Cricket Club; I thought I might possibly manage to catch a glimpse of a fielder through the tiered seating. The filthy courtyard in the centre of the block was a sordid contrast to the elegance and luxury of the flats themselves. Servants working for the wealthy residents lived there with their wives and children, sleeping, cooking and washing in cramped and squalid conditions. The walls were crumbling and stained with the excrement of pigeons, constantly dripping air-conditioners, overflowing drainpipes and green mould, the result of heavy monsoon rains. At night-time the staircase landings and passages were full of sleeping bodies. Every morning a vegetable vendor visited, selling tomatoes, onions, carrots, cucumbers, green beans, cabbage, aubergines and ladies' fingers. In the elevator there was a sign in bold lettering, 'Servants are not allowed to use the lift', so he carried a large basket on his head and ascended the eight floors via the dark central stairway where the steps were broken and cracked and a stench of urine pervaded the air.

The furnishings of the Gordhondases' spacious apartment were a mixture of the expensive and the cheap. A torn and frayed carpet covered the mottled tiled floor of the living room. There were glass-topped side-tables and a formica table, a Rajasthani cloth-painting hanging along one of the dark wood-panelled walls and two sofas covered in brown plastic arranged in front of a large Sony video set. On display were mementos from foreign travels including ornate Venetian handblown goblets and a collection of books, most of which were in English, including American pulp paperbacks and the *Encyclopaedia Britannica*. Four bedrooms led from the central living area and over each door hung a plait of mango leaves, a symbol of good luck. The kitchen, approached by a rear entrance, was small and airless. Although the interior of the apartment was kept spotlessly clean, the balcony on which they performed their puja was filthy. The walls were painted blue and were smeared with dirt and coloured paints and a pile of old newspapers was stacked in one corner.

Mr Gordhondas's mother lived with them until five years ago when, finding city life too hectic, she made her home in a small bungalow set in a large garden full of wheat and sugar-cane, not far from one of the family textile mills near Kanpur in Uttar Pradesh. Despite her fondness and respect for the old woman, Kamala felt relief at her departure. A deeply devout and traditional lady, she had rigidly adhered to cleansing rituals that were both exhausting and impractical. She refused to allow soap in her bathroom, insisting that a jar of mud was placed by the washbasin and the toilet. She insisted, too, that the kitchen utensils were scoured with a handful of sand, and she refused to eat off china plates.

'We now use modern household cleaners but my mother-in-law thought they were impure. Even today when she visits we do it her way just for the sake of peace.

'While her husband was still alive she washed his feet for him every morning and went through a giddy ritual of bending down and touching them a hundred and eight times, a number corresponding to the beads on a rosary. She prayed to him as if he were an idol of her own god. When he died, my husband and his brothers removed all their mother's jewellery and she had her hair cut very short. Now she no longer wears the tilaka on her forehead and always wears white saris, keeping her head covered at all times. Her beautiful handwoven silk saris were distributed among her daughters.'

After her husband's death she handed over her responsibilities as head of the household to Kamala and prepared to devote her final years to a life of devotion. Sometimes, when she found certain aspects of her husband's habits unbearable, Kamala had confided in the old lady.

'She seemed mildly sympathetic but always advised me that it was my duty as a wife to cope with any problems rather than confront them. She had very little education and never analysed anyone's behaviour as I do. Also it was easy for her to talk like that because she was married to a very good man. I really envied her that. My father-in-law was utterly devoted to her and begrudged her nothing.'

Before his own marriage Ranjit Gordhondas had traded in cloth and had then decided to manufacture his own. To be a mill owner was extremely prestigious, and certainly enhanced his prospects of making a fine marriage. His family bought for him a textile mill in Worli, a large industrial centre north of the city, which I went to visit early in my acquaintance with the family. The mill was an old-fashioned one-storey building constructed of wood. The offices were situated in a pleasant central courtyard full of exotic plants, and pigeons and crows nested behind the splintered shutters and awning frames. By contrast there were abandoned cars, tethered buffaloes and small forges in the surrounding streets. Set back were rows of wooden one-room dwellings. The ground was drenched by the crowded water pumps leaving a residue of thick black mud in which babies crawled, children played, and pigs and warthogs slumbered. Scores of families had made their homes on the pavements, congregating in small enclaves known as bustees, hoping that they might get a job in the mill.

Ranjit Gordhondas's looms produced a variety of cloths including printed chintzes for furnishings and a range of luxury bed linens.

'We have sixty-two thousand spindles on the premises and nine hundred looms, producing sixty-five thousand metres of cloth every day. There are over two thousand workers, both Hindu and Muslim. It's like a small state and I am the appointed dictator!' he beamed at me as he slowly cracked his fingers. The workers were chiefly migrants coming from the states of Uttar Pradesh, Maharashtra and Bihar. It was a calculated risk to bring one's family to Bombay with its reputation of being the most wealthy city in the country. They did not come from nearby Bhiwandi, traditional home of loom workers, because there they were only trained to work on handlooms, not the mechanised units.

'We pay our workers up to fifty rupees per day. In Bhiwandi that's what they are paid in one week,' he boasted.

'Recently I purchased some land north of the airport, seventeen acres in all, where I hope to construct some housing, although I can see that with the corruption in operation in the planning department I will probably have to pay a bribe to get started. I also have two barrel factories, manufacturing containers for carrying oil – one here and one in Calcutta. All the time we are expanding and yet at the same time finding new ways of economising and cutting down on expenses. Already I have set up branches of our textile services in Lucknow and Kanpur, which means I am constantly on the move.'

He went on to tell me that Ashish's desire to study medicine caused him great pain which was matched by his scepticism when the young man fell in love with a girl outside their community. On the other hand, when he came to his senses, maybe they could set up a pharmaceutical business together. Ranjit wanted Santanu to come and work with him as soon as he had completed his accountancy studies.

He inherited from his father a small film studio which is now hired out to make advertising commercials. In the past, successful business men often acquired a studio as a diversion from manufacturing. They would be cautious of introducing their sons into that area of their business, however, as the glamour could corrupt and distract them from their traditional Marwari obligations.

16 In Calcutta a Marwari housewife performs puja on her balcony   17 A Marwari wedding gift, typically decked in rupee notes   18 Apprehension shows on the bride's face   19 Relief that the ceremony is over

Ranjit Gorhondas talked with energy and pride of his wide range of interests and activities. 'I'm involved in various organisations in the city. I'm a director of the Nehru Centre. They control a planetarium, an exhibition centre and an auditorium, but it's a tough job to remain in this city and to keep going. It's difficult enough just trying to manage one's own affairs let alone satisfy one's philanthropic instincts. To operate in the political arena one has to fraternise with politicians and their demands don't suit good people. I'm happy at my mill so why should I kow-tow to someone in power simply to hop on to a corrupt bandwagon? Marwaris of my grandfather's generation made a much greater contribution to the general welfare of the public than they do now. They believed in living simply and seemed to understand human and environmental problems, building schools and hospitals. They wanted to do something for the cities in which they settled, but that has changed. People today who make money spend so much on themselves there's no money left to give.'

I was confused by this unexpected pang of social conscience. Ranjit Gordhondas's view of his ancestors' social commitment was tinged with a hint of sentimentality. Marwaris had always performed what they called their religious duty to society in an ostentatious manner. The lavish temples they built and the charitable endowments they made enhanced their personal status.

There was a hint of irony as he expounded his philosophies, seated in air-conditioned comfort wearing a dazzling white, freshly laundered cotton kurta pyjama outfit. When I asked him about his opinions of the caste system he replied unhesitatingly.

'I don't believe in casteism at all. Period. It's a man-made evil which evolved through custom. I'm sure that in the time of Adam and Eve there were neither Brahmins nor Untouchables. For myself, I believe you should only ever do something because it's what you want to do, not just out of a sense of duty and tradition. My own personal discipline is to take myself in hand when I feel I am becoming depressed. People tend not to like it if I'm unhappy so if I'm sad I tend to hide it. As you can see, I'm not a typical Marwari. I could never be branded as such.'

To be fair, Ranjit Gordhondas's denial that he was a 'typical' Marwari was partially justified. Neither he nor his wife displayed

20 A fifteen-year-old Marwari girl preparing for her engagement party wears a sari for the first time

their wealth in a particularly ostentatious manner, even though they were preoccupied with retaining and increasing it. Although Kamala wore a ring with a large pear-shaped diamond on her wedding finger and an ornate gold watch, the designs were tastefully modest. She had established quite a reputation for herself as a shrewd business-woman in her own right. Nearly fifteen years earlier she had set up a small trading house, buying and selling manufactured steel structures. It was a surprising commodity for a woman, especially an Indian Marwari, to involve herself with, but when all her children were in full-time schooling she resolved to find herself some occupation. Coming from a family of industrialists, living-room conversation had always been concerned with the world of business. She felt her knowledge of trade was so much greater than her knowledge of philanthropic affairs that inaugurating her own small company seemed a logical step.

Kamala had a small office situated on the fifth floor of a rambling old block close to the central Victoria Terminus. The lift seldom worked and the office itself lacked the space and comfort of her apartment on Marine Drive. It was shabbily furnished in clashing shades of green. On mail boxes in the main lobby were printed the names of the other business concerns operating in the same building, including petro-chemical and steel-casting agents, private detectives, tea companies, manufacturers of chemicals and plywood oil mills, electronic firms, rubber companies, and many others. Beside the entrance there was a counter selling tea, coffee, onion and cheese pakoras and vegetable cutlets alongside a doorless men's urinal from which emanated a stale and putrid stench. Kamala was the sole director in her own company which boasted a healthy annual turnover. However, she did not work with her husband's blessing.

'I really think she was happier when she was looking after me and the children,' he complained, 'but when they started to grow up she became a little bored and restless. In the last couple of years there's been a real change in her. Apart from suffering from the high blood pressure, she seems worried and agitated. Maybe she didn't choose a suitable market. She should have gone into ladies' or children's wear. But I think her real place is in the home and that is where she should have remained.'

Kamala struggled to maintain a calm and unruffled exterior. She constantly battled between what was traditionally expected of her and her own inner emotions. Her personality was a mixture of contradictions and I noticed how her facial expression often reflected an internal fight. In repose she furrowed her brow as though troubled by her thoughts, but, sidetracked, her face lit up as she smiled and laughed. She emphatically stated that she was always trying to see the best in what was around her, constantly weighing up the good and bad points. While I was staying with the family I would often accompany Kamala to her office. Traffic conditions in Bombay were appalling but this allowed us plenty of time to talk as we sat together in the back of her chauffeur-driven car.

'It's difficult for me to say when I was really happy. I grew up in Hyderabad and as a girl I studied classical dance but after my marriage I never had a chance to do it again. Of course there have been good moments but basically I am a worrier. I'm getting to know myself quite well so now if I find myself worrying too much about something I can't do very much about, I will concentrate harder on my work or organising some form of outing with my friends. That way I give myself less time to worry.

'I feel it is important to get away sometimes, just to find oneself and what one's real strengths are. I spent two months last summer travelling all over Europe and the US. I began with a cruise of the Greek Islands and then visited Rome, Paris and London before going to visit relatives in Canada and New York. I'm not sure when I'll be able to travel like that again.'

Since she had started working on her own she had found that she was easily bored by her Marwari contemporaries and craved companionship and stimulus from women outside her community.

'When I become friendly with another woman, I don't think I am really looking for a particular quality, but I like the company of people I can communicate with and inevitably I find I have more in common with people like myself who are working. I didn't choose my husband or my children, although their welfare is important to me, but you choose your friends and they are very much a part of my well-being and happiness. It isn't so easy to pursue friendships because at home I have to give all my time to attend to my husband's needs. I would like to do more for society at large, women especially, maybe setting up a training scheme so they can work. Here, in Bombay, many have a very raw deal. Frequently deserted by their husbands who don't share the responsibility of the children, few have skills to survive such hardships. Even in my privileged position, this can be a chaotic city. One is constantly battling with traffic jams, telephones not working, power cuts, strikes, gas shortages and the like.'

One evening when I was dining at the Gymkhana Club with Ashish and Rithu, Ashish expressed his cynicism for his mother's intentions to assist those less fortunate than herself. 'We once helped to organise a charity concert for flood victims and she said she was too busy to help. When she makes small contributions it's just to appease her conscience.' Yet I thought his judgment harsh, especially in the light of his own change of heart since he first became a doctor. Despite her efforts and protestations, her behaviour was a paradox. She denied that she had ever touched alcohol, but at times she had been seen drinking cognac, VSOP, a black market luxury. But coming to terms with living in a city where thousands sleep every night on the pavements and where the cost of a silk sari can feed a whole family for a year created conflict for any caring person living in comfort.

I soon became aware of how Kamala's life still revolved around her children, as would be expected of any affectionate Hindu mother. She was at the centre of the home, everyone depending on her to organise all household matters. Although Shalini would soon be leaving home, she regarded both Rithu and Premula as her own daughters. She knew that no home is big enough for more than one mature woman, but, as each Marwari wife was preoccupied with pleasing her husband, a calm surface was always maintained.

'Until they start their own families I am keeping them busy and making sure they don't get bored. I delegate certain household duties to them both and sometimes they come to the office and do some work for me, addressing envelopes, filing and the like. As long as they are living under my roof I am responsible for them.'

Every Monday morning Kamala Gordhondas made a detour on her way to her office and visited a beauty parlour on Malabar Hill. The proprietress, Mrs Mirchandini, although elegant in appearance, had a warm and reassuring personality. She explained to me that many of her clients visited her not so much to have treatment but because within sympathetic surroundings they were able to verbally unburden themselves of their personal frustrations.

'Fifty per cent of my clients are Marwari and many of them use this place as a refuge from the suffocating atmosphere of their homes. You see, so many of them are deeply unhappy. It starts very early in their lives because when their marriages are arranged they are married off as commodities and what the girl herself feels doesn't matter. It is an interconnection between two business houses.

'Rarely is a Marwari bride allowed to pursue a career after marriage. She may even have studied law but she won't be allowed to practise. She will have to be a dutiful 'daughter', and the only social life she has will be to accompany her mother-in-law and to participate in their religious customs.

'Young husbands have a freedom their wives don't have and he only takes her out when it suits him. One notices that in their teens girls are discouraged from mixing with their friends from school. They are being prepared to be obedient wives. A girl may have worn jeans and sweaters at college but after marriage she will always have to wear a sari and keep her head covered in the presence of her elders. In time, when a bride is further tied by a young family, her husband will become unfaithful. These young men now want another kind of woman, young starlets, models and the like, and because they have money they can pay any price. When a Marwari girl is married she can never go back to her parents' home. The family would be ostracised by their own community to such an extent it would be too much for them to bear.'

Kamala told me that no Marwari husband was faithless to his wife, but she knew this was an ostrich-like belief. She comforted herself with the words 'Hear no evil, see no evil'. Ranjit Gordhondas had business interests in several cities. Kamala knew it was likely that in each he kept a mistress but she was unable to do anything about it and it would be unthinkable for her to do the same thing. So much of her unhappiness as she approached middle age was frustration at being unable to please her husband and the fact that her own children's need for her was diminishing as they grew up. It was Kamala's resolution to pursue her own business interests which ultimately saved her from the despair suffered by many of her Marwari contemporaries.

'Yes, maybe I am disappointed with much of my married life,' she confided one evening while I was sitting on the floor of her bedroom watching her fix her sari. 'I can't push or coax my husband into anything. If I try he only rebels, so if I want my way I have to try subtler means. More than anything I wanted to walk with him in life. Even today I am still trying to see if there could be some way we could develop a companionship. When there are difficulties, when I feel distanced from him, I try hard not to pester him. I believe one has to accept things the way they are rather than create new problems. As I have travelled to Western countries, I have seen that it's not the same there. There's so much talk of permissiveness; it's a sorry state of affairs. Everything is regarded as physical but where is the spiritual, the solace? I think people keep changing partners in the hope of finding peace of mind. For me the most important thing in a relationship is to feel mentally at ease with one another because the physical desire will fade.' As she talks she is perhaps aware that she has the same desires as her Western counterpart but here, within her community, the rules and forfeits are so different.

Ranjit Gordhondas had a favourite proverb: if you eat chicken at home, then you desire to go out and eat dal. Marwaris are vegetarian and dal, made from boiled spiced lentils, was usually served with every meal. Within the home he rigorously adhered to a strict code of behaviour but he sometimes ate meat, smoked cigarettes and drank alcohol while away from his family. He had a niece who suffered polio in early infancy and had to be taken to a special restaurant to eat cheese and eggs, forbidden foods which contained the protein necessary to strengthen her bones.

At seven o'clock each morning a servant came into the bedroom Ranjit shared with his wife with a tray of tea. At half-past seven the pandit, the family priest, came to their flat. He relinquished his leather shoes at the threshold, as the dead flesh was a symbol of pollution and untouchability. He then said prayers on the balcony for almost forty minutes, lighting candles, quoting mantras and performing arti. He rang a small bell while he chanted. As they awoke the family joined him, each for a few minutes, and then they ate their breakfast.

'The pandit's daily presence is important as a reminder of one's religious duty in life and of the sanctity of the family home,' explained Kamala. The Gordhondases paid him 100 rupees per month plus his breakfast. When he had finished in their household he visited another, serving a total of ten families.

Kamala performed puja twice daily, sitting cross-legged on the floor in front of the shrine. The bindi marks of red powder pressed on to her forehead symbolised a third eye, that of intellect and wisdom. The offerings made while arti was performed included a handful of coins, this being a Marwari household. Kamala always encouraged Shalini and her daughters-in-law to sit with her during this ceremony but her husband and sons tended to make only a token gesture, a small touch of the forehead as they mumbled a greeting to their priest. However, for the first four days of their periods the women were not allowed on to the balcony to say their prayers. Unaccustomed to such an attitude through her own upbringing, Rithu was quite embarrassed by it. 'It's because all the servants know about one's condition. I know one is regarded as being in an unclean state but quite honestly I think it was a tradition invented by women. Men are so lazy on the whole that this was a way in which we could just get a few days' rest each month.'

Every weekday Rithu and Premula went to Crawford Market to buy fruit and vegetables, making a note of every rupee spent. Kamala explained, 'I advise them both how to set about doing the shopping, how to maintain the household accounts and prepare the menu for meals. We keep a very close watch on what we spend on groceries and we do one large shop for basic provisions once a month. If we run short of cash we realise that either we have been entertaining too much or something is going wrong in the kitchen.'

Every Sunday lunchtime they had open house for all their relatives living in Bombay and to economise would seriously dent Kamala's reputation as a fine and generous hostess. On Saturday afternoons she oversaw activities in the kitchen. The cook prepared a variety of vegetable curries, lentil pancakes with yoghurt, a traditional Rajasthani dish of dried sangar (similar to a runner bean or ladies' finger), rice, sugared lentils with almonds, stuffed chapattis, puris and popadums and a sweet dish of milk mixed with cottage cheese and sugar-cane. On the Sunday morning two Brahmins were invited into the kitchen to taste the dishes before they were put out on to the dining table, as an act of purification. The women sometimes fasted and for each of them a plate with slices of fresh fruit, papaya, lime, apple and watermelon, was prepared, which they always ate first to avoid pollution.

The Gordhondas had four servants who came from Bihar and Uttar Pradesh; they made the long trip home once a year for a month's leave. Experience had taught the Gordhondases not to employ anyone living in their home state of Maharashtra as he would regularly present excuses to make short visits to his village. Two men worked in the kitchen and the other two were responsible for keeping the home clean and serving at table. They sent their salaries of 250 rupees a month (about £15) back home to their families and were provided with accommodation, food, clothing and medication. Kamala thought they were underpaid but blamed the system. They had one girl servant who was on duty from seven o'clock in the morning until early evening. Her duties included mending, ironing and dusting, and when she was not working she squatted in a corner of the living room in readiness for any small task that should arise.

Kamala claimed never to have asked a prospective servant about his caste but she could pick up instinctively on his background by his dress and behaviour. They employed only Hindus in the home. Every morning the Jamadai (a Harijan) came to clean the toilets. As soon as he had left the apartment one of the other servants would clean with a cloth where he had trodden.

None of the servants had any home in the city. They kept their few personal items and uniforms in a small utility room behind the kitchen and slept on a mat – on the balcony in the dry months and on the kitchen floor or on the landing of the apartment block during the rainy season. They had no complaints. They all knew that they were the lucky ones, having employment and the security of a regular income with which they could support their families.

In Kamala's opinion the most valuable quality of Hinduism was tolerance. 'Everyone is free to choose for themselves. Each of us can choose our own interpretation of the Gita and the Vedas. Our way of life is an acceptance of the circumstances into which we are born.

80

I believe absolutely in one's karma, one's fate. The most important thing is to do what we feel is our duty and I'm not sure we really need a temple or a priest for that.'

Her faith was a vital prop in her everyday life so she was never at a loss for words when discussing the many facets of Hinduism.

'In my parents' house, Hanuman [the monkey god] and Shiva were worshipped. Although I started to worship Durga when I got married I don't think it makes any difference. One is basically praying to one supreme being. I think if someone says he is an atheist he must be a very fearless person. He must have so much confidence to survive without a support system. I look for guidance from somewhere above. When I pray I ask for the continued welfare of my family, to be a better human being and to have peace within myself.

'I know the pandit comes to the flat every day but I don't think religious rites in themselves are so important. It's a custom my mother-in-law believed in and I don't see anything actually wrong in it. There's no harm after one has bathed in the morning to give at least two or three minutes' thought to religion, so it's fine with me. It is a brief whisper of mental discipline I suppose, interrupting our more mundane preoccupations. However, when I travel I don't perform my puja. Within myself I can usually work out what is right and what is wrong.'

Twice a year Kamala observed a nine-day sacrament when she performed special prayers for the goddess Durga. A clay model idol was daily presented with flowers, leaves and food. On the eighth day a fire was lit, a symbol of purity and a sign to thank the gods for visiting the home. Throughout this period she avoided all cereals, rice, wheat and onions and only ate one meal a day, believing that physical sacrifice was good for the soul. It made pleasure more pleasurable.

Shalini Gordhondas's marriage to Jayanti Kumar took place three months after their engagement party. He had kept in touch, telephoning her once a week from Madras, but the connection had usually been very poor and their conversations brief and stilted. Over five hundred relatives and friends were invited and five days of sumptuous banquets and traditional ceremonies were planned. To the devout the only celebrations of true religious significance were the Ganesh puja and the Phere. During the Ganesh puja prayers were made, requesting all obstacles to be removed so that the marriage could take place with an open mind and a clear conscience. The Phere was the climax of the marriage ceremony when seven vows of mutual commitment were made.

It was because of the Marwaris' origins in Rajasthan that there were so many days of celebration. Two centuries ago, travelling across the desert to attend a wedding necessitated a considerable amount of time and planning, so marriages were extended over many days to allow time for the families to relax and enjoy themselves after the strenuous journey. These days, the redundant ceremonies provide an excuse to flaunt wealth to friends and relations. On the way to the reception at the Bombay Oberoi Hotel the bride's uncle grumbled, 'It's really obscene, the magnitude of this present giving.' His wife retorted, 'This is a once in a lifetime event which is why we like to do it in great style.' Many of the guests found it inconvenient to attend a wedding late in June, a time when they would normally be taking their annual vacations, but attendance was a family duty and great offence would be taken if the invitation was refused.

The opening family puja was a simple affair. Shalini, her parents and brothers and their own pandit gathered together on their balcony to say the special prayer to the elephant god, Ganesh.

At the first major ceremony, the Tika, held in a conference hall on Sunday morning, all male guests from both sides were present but only the ladies from the groom's family. Gifts were offered and accepted: baskets of mangoes, cherries, lychees and almonds, and another full of imported confectionery – Toblerone, Polomints and Wrigley's chewing-gum. There were trays of toiletries, suits, clocks, silver salvers, teapots, a Sony tape deck, gentlemen's shirts and much more, all laid out on a raised platform behind which hung a photograph of the groom's deceased grandfather, garlanded with a necklace of orange and yellow marigolds. Such garlands are only ever laid over photographs of deceased relatives. Beside the buffet table, piles of cardboard boxes full of sweet delicacies and covered with bright paper were stacked, to be distributed to departing guests. The hall was full, all the guests had arrived and they impatiently waited for the Brahmin priests to start the proceedings. 'We have to go by the priests' watch, not ours!' I heard someone joke.

When Tika was completed, the groom touched all the ladies' feet in a gesture of greetings and thanks. Then the guests formed an orderly queue, headed by the women – large, bespectacled and swathed in fabulous brightly coloured silk saris – and they were served the first of many exotic vegetarian meals, accompanied by fruit squash and mango lassi. Alcohol is never served at an official Marwari feast.

That afternoon, in the Gordhondases' apartment, the ladies had mehndi, intricate patterns painted with a paste of henna and lime, deftly drawn on to their hands and feet by a lady from the Vayshya subcaste of Misramis. The markings on the back of the hand were for their brothers and those on the palm for the well-being of their husbands. Shalini began to dress in her parents' bedroom while her aunts and small cousins drifted in and out of the room. While she was seated at her mother's dressing-table all the women took a hand in arranging her hair, changing the style and adjusting the headdress. Ranjit Gordhondas lay on the bed reading out loud his brother's horoscope.

Outwardly, Shalini was approaching her marriage with a spirit of enthusiasm, but inwardly she was frightened and apprehensive of what lay ahead – a new life in a new city living among strangers. She seemed to enjoy, however, the warmth generated in her parents' flat by her relatives, and found being the centre of attention exciting. In the living room the women had their own, less ornate, ceremony of handing over gifts: saris for the bride, cosmetics, silver costume jewellery and bangles. The most lavish gifts were laid out in Shalini's bedroom. There was even a paper aeroplane constructed with over seven hundred 1-rupee notes.

During the evening, in the basement ballroom suite of the Oberoi, the Bhat Nutna was held, in which Kamala Gordhondas formally invited her own brothers and their families to her daughter's wedding. As a gesture of hospitality and affection, water was sprinkled on the feet of the groom's party as they arrived. This was strictly a family affair but the network of aunts, uncles and cousins amounted to nearly two hundred people. They came in one large group, already dragging their feet a little, prematurely weary of the days of ritual and over-eating ahead. Kamala then spoon-fed the brothers with rice, green cereal and vegetables. The three grown men found themselves giggling at the absurdity of this ritual and they shook with suppressed laughter as she pressed vermilion powder and rice on to their foreheads. Two large rats suddenly appeared and chased each other over the thick-pile carpet to a chorus of applause from the assembled company. 'Look, five-star rats having a merry time!'

Jayanti chatted to his brothers, occasionally glancing at Shalini who, for a time, nonchalantly pretended to ignore him. Then their eyes met and he beckoned her over to his side and led her to the head table. They both appeared calm and relaxed but as all eyes were on them they could do little more than exchange small talk.

Monday was the day of Hald Haath, an informal day of intricate, intimate family ceremonies, most of which were enacted by the women. A small shrine had been set up beside the Gordhondases' large antiquated fridge which creaked and groaned in a corner of the dining room. The women took it in turns to say their prayers while the men breakfasted. While the wives prepared to guide Shalini through a sequence of symbolic rites, the husbands, many of them resplendent in their beautifully cut starched white kurta pyjamas, flipped through the pages of business and sports magazines. Most professed to finding these ceremonies a waste of time and yet were secretly grateful for a few days' enforced rest from their business activities. The heavy monsoon rains had just begun so they were unable to relieve the tedium with short walks along the sea shore.

Janak Goenka, Kamala's younger brother, a somewhat eccentric gentleman who was often regarded as the black sheep of the family, enjoyed holding forth on the female of the species. 'Women are just a distraction. For men, life outside the home is the most important. His family are merely a cushion in the background. His wife would be wrong to expect him to take any real interest in either her or their children. I'm quite delighted for my brother-in-law that he is getting his daughter married. It will get her out of the way!'

Nobody rose to his bait, knowing that to argue would only indulge him. During one particular rite, when Kamala was having her hair combed and plaited, Janak Goenka kept hovering in the doorway making provocative remarks.

'Okay,' shrieked the women. 'If you want to join in let's marry you to your sister.' Amidst peals of laughter Kamala's sari was pulled over her face, her brother dragged into the room and led through a mock ceremony.

'Okay. Point taken. I give in,' he cried as he was ushered away and told to find an audience for his ranting among the men.

On the eve of the wedding day, a dinner was given for the bride's family by a relative who headed a large shipping concern. The word 'informal' was printed on the invitation but the enormous house on Malabar Hill was so opulent it could hardly lend itself to an intimate gathering. The reception room was the size of a small ballroom with vast couches and seats stiffly arranged in one long row. The most modern Japanese hi-fi and video equipment was built into ornately carved mahogany units. The ladies sat together on one side of the room and the gentlemen gathered on the other, a custom which had evolved from the men wishing to discuss business among themselves.

On the morning of the wedding day the family priest arrived at the apartment shortly before eight o'clock and Shalini was put through another round of rituals. The first was a Marwari social custom. A pink sari was held over her head while she sat down and stretched out her hands and feet for blessing. Then her brothers and uncles splashed her hair and face with fronds of grass dipped in haldi, turmeric and oil, all herbal products used in beauty treatment. Finally her father poured yoghurt over the hapless girl's head. Even though Shalini then had to take a shower and wash her hair it was all treated like a pantomime with a good sense of fun. There was no religious significance to any of this. It was simply a tradition dating back to the desert life of their Marwari ancestors. Bathing was difficult owing to shortage of water so these unctions were used to cleanse the bride.

'These ladies are inventing the fifth Veda for their amusement. We don't need women's liberation in this country because this is it,' joked Janak Goenka, but they were becoming irritated by his ridicule.

Then Shalini changed yet again and prepared herself to leave her home for the last time as an unmarried girl. As she looked around her room, at the familiar furnishings and pictures, she felt a small knot of panic twist inside her stomach, but her mother, sensing her fear and unease, gripped her hand tightly and without saying a word led her to the front door.

All the ladies took themselves to a suite at the Taj Hotel where Shalini underwent a two-hour session with a woman who specialised in painting young girls' faces for their weddings. The pink bridal outfit, costing over 7,000 rupees, was a gift from her maternal uncles. Its full skirt, bodice and sari were elaborately embroidered with flowers in gold, silver and jade-green thread. She would only wear it once; then it would be stored and brought out only to be shown to her children. She would also be able to show them the video of the wedding. Videos had proved extremely popular if only as a record of the lavish and extravagant spending.

Again all the women tried to adjust Shalini's outfit. One of her aunts kept telling her to relax but it wasn't easy wearing an outfit that weighed nearly 5 kilos. Her mother attached a red thread with coloured cotton balls around her neck and a bracelet of shells linked with scarlet cotton around her ankle, symbols to ward off the evil eye which would be removed by her husband as soon as they were married. Then Kamala hung a magnificent diamond necklace around her neck, her own personal wedding gift, before they all went down to the banqueting hall.

It was a moving sight when the groom and his family made their entrance. The rain was pouring down and a gusty wind swept across the bay as a group of elderly gentlemen played their ancient and tuneless trumpets and clarinets. A drummer beat out a strong rhythm as Jayanti's friends and brothers formed a small circle and bowed their heads in a traditional dance. They led in the young man, perilously perched on the rump of a frisky white horse festooned with coloured ribbons and feathers.

Jayanti clearly looked nervous and uncomfortable in his white suit of close-fitting jacket and tight trousers with a scarlet and yellow Rajasthani-style turban. He gratefully slipped off the horse and was ushered up a grandly sweeping staircase to the ballroom. As future man and wife were led towards each other, the laughing guests showered them with scarlet rose petals. Ranjit Gordhondas had ordered that no expense should be spared to adorn the enormous ballroom but the proceedings began amidst farcical scenes of disorganisation. As the guests gathered, workmen were still busy decorating the wedding arbour, the mandapan, with trails of white blooms interlaced with red carnations, asters and coloured fairy lights. There was also a large backdrop panel of flowers with a portrait of Ganesh picked out in bright orange French marigolds in front of which the newly married couple would receive their guests. Shalini's elderly grandmother confided that she didn't really enjoy weddings.

'No one does really. It is tradition which compels us to go through with it and our community always enjoys an excuse to show off its financial strength. If Shalini had wanted to avoid having a wedding on this scale she would have had to have the urge and the initiative to rebel. What one may want for oneself may not be possible because the groom's family would want it this way. However, by Marwari standards this is a simple affair. When I married the arrangements were four times as lavish.'

A Hindu wedding ceremony can take half an hour to perform or be extended over four hours, according to the couple's wishes. Despite the complexity of the rituals, no rehearsal was needed. Since childhood both Shalini and Jayanti had regularly attended wedding ceremonies. For nearly two hours, they sat with their Brahmin priests and their parents under the mandapan, while the guests strolled around the ballroom, read newspapers, drank tea, ate pan and betelnut and chattered among themselves. The climax of the ceremony, the Phere, was reached when Jayanti led his bride seven times around a small fire which had been lit as the gods' chief witness. Each time they encircled the flame they made a different promise to each other, while the priests chanted a series of mantras.

After the seventh circle they sat down, changing seats. They were now legally man and wife and Jayanti pressed a red bindi mark on to the forehead of his new wife. The main ceremony completed, the couple made a small puja together at a simple shrine set up behind the flowered arbour. They then returned to their seats and untied the coloured cotton strands from each other's wrists and ankles, a simple and friendly game in which they publicly made one another's acquaintance. As he fiddled with a tight knot Shalini could see that Jayanti was both shaking and sweating profusely so she reached up and relieved him of his heavily jewelled headdress.

With the marriage ceremony completed, Jayanti left to take a shower and change into more comfortable clothing, a grey Western-style lounge suit. Shalini had to remain in her bridal attire for the photographic portraits. The photo session lasted nearly two hours, as long as the wedding ceremony itself, with every guest being photographed individually with the bride and groom. Meanwhile a lavish buffet was served, although some guests slipped away as soon as they had been photographed without bothering to wait for the final ceremony.

At last Shalini was allowed to change into another outfit, a stunning gold and scarlet sari, and then rejoined the celebrations to make a final public puja to her family goddess, Durga. She and Jayanti went through the motions of eating a symbolic first meal together before she was taken to join his family and introduced to their family god and goddess, Ram and Sita. Her cousins and aunts began to weep now that they were losing her for ever. As she was clasped in a warm embrace by her uncles and father, Shalini too broke down. But then this emotional reaction was to be expected. Many times in the past Shalini had seen a new bride break down thus and she was responding to the occasion. Jayanti, with seemingly genuine affection, put his arm gently around her shoulder and led her down the stairs to a waiting limousine. From Kamala there were no tears – just a smile of relief and satisfaction. Her duty had been done, her daughter satisfactorily married and the promise of an extended network of business secured.

Fifteen months later I met Shalini in Madras at the home of her new family. To her delight, she had found living with Jayanti, his parents and sisters much more relaxed than she had anticipated. Although her father-in-law was ruthless in his business affairs, at home the family were less rigorous than her own in maintaining Marwari traditions. Her mother-in-law did all the cooking, enlisting the help of her daughters and Shalini, and there was only one servant who was responsible for all the household chores including cleaning the washrooms. She visited Bombay for Diwali, and, although pleased to see her mother and Rithu, she found the tensions and formal behaviour irksome. After only a few days she was eager to return to her new husband. Shortly after her marriage she enrolled at a college in the city, intending to embark on an economics degree, but on becoming pregnant abandoned the course after one term. We had tea together one month before her child was due. She chatted happily about her life, the friends she had made, the pleasure she took in caring for Jayanti and how the anticipation of becoming a mother thrilled her. If arranged marriages are indeed a 'lucky dip', then she had put in her hand and pulled out a diamond brooch.

5

A Weaver's Family in Andhra Pradesh

O n one of my visits to Bombay I took my four-year-old son
with me. Having spent some time there, we flew to Delhi and
from there I intended to proceed to Andhra Pradesh, the large state
in the centre of southern India. I wanted to visit the village where I
had worked for Christian Aid, to introduce my child to the villagers
with whom I had kept in touch and to talk to a family of weavers.
We could have flown to the nearest city, Hyderabad, but I thought
my young English nanny should see something of the countryside and
experience travelling on the Indian railways. In the past I have
been in both the most luxurious compartments and in the most
crowded and uncomfortable conditions but for this trip I decided
that the three of us would enjoy the journey most if I secured berths
in an air-conditioned sleeper. I knew that most Indians have to make
their bookings weeks in advance, but some spaces are held in reserve
for government officials so I enlisted the help of a member of the
Legislative Assembly I had met at a dinner party. Writing on his
headed notepaper I put in a request to the terminus manager for three
seats and discovered for the first time the vagaries of the corrupt and
complicated bureaucratic system. Within a few minutes I was given
permission to travel on the train of my choice.

The journey to Hyderabad took nearly eighteen hours. Fortunately
my nanny had the foresight to provide some entertainment. She had

purchased packets of balloons which we blew up and hung in bunches from the reading lights. Then, to the amusement and mirth of our fellow passengers, she unravelled some rolls of toilet paper, twisting and draping the tissue like Christmas decorations around the overhead luggage racks. There were candles, too, which we lit when it got dark, balancing them on a large chunk of peanut brittle instead of a cake. My son was delighted and I was grateful for the diversion.

After spending a few days in Hyderabad recovering from the journey we drove 40 miles through the stony and inhospitable landscape north of the city. The scattered villages appeared like welcome small green oases in a barren land. Large pylons, recently constructed to conduct hydro-electricity to outlying areas, were the only visible sign of India moving towards the twenty-first century. It was neither desert nor pasture, although herds of undernourished buffaloes could be seen munching at dried-out shrubs, their ribs shining through their dark hides like black metal cages. All along the roadside grew thick thorny bushes of a plant introduced by the British during a serious fuel shortage in about 1910. It is hardy and fast growing and, like the toddy palm, thrives on little water.

Cheemalkondor was a well-organised community of about two thousand inhabitants, with a village headman, or Sarpanch, elected by the upper castes. As well as agriculturalists, shepherds, weavers, potters, store keepers, dhobis (washermen), basket makers, tailors, carpenters, blacksmiths, barbers, cobblers and one goldsmith all making a living there, two communities of Harijans were settled outside the village boundary. These were the Mala, a scheduled caste which had inherited the traditional role of handling all forms of dead flesh, and the Madiga, who laboured on the land. There were also four Muslim families who lived alongside the Harijan communities and thirty Roman Catholic families who resided in a small unit of sturdily built houses about a quarter of a mile from the village centre.

An electrical supply was installed in the village some five years ago but it reached only about ten homes. There was no proper drainage system, and approach to the village from the asphalt highway 2 miles away was made by a very uneven sandy cart path. A small store sold basic essentials, such as tea, sugar, kerosene and soap, and three temples catered for the needs of the various castes. In the village school there was one primary and one kindergarten teacher who gave the children up to the age of twelve basic instruction in reading, writing, health care, mathematics and social science. An attendance fee of 2 rupees daily (about 10 pence) was charged, and all the children sat and mingled together, irrespective of their castes. Yet only a hundred or so inhabitants of the village could read and write fluently, all of them male. When the school was first opened some thirty years earlier, it was regarded with suspicion. What was the government's intention, to feed the minds of children in this way? Everyone had survived hitherto without being able to read and write.

Caste Hindus made up three-quarters of the community. There were twelve fresh-water wells at their disposal, and a further thirty wells with water suitable for irrigational purposes. The Harijan and Muslim families had only two wells.

One farmer opted to act as the postman, and allowed his living quarters to be used as a post office for an hour every morning. On the rare occasion when a Harijan wanted to send a letter, he had to stand outside the front entrance to make his request for a stamp and then hand over his money and the envelope from outside the threshold. There was no medically qualified person living in the village although one family practised the traditional ayurvedic medicine and operated a small private dispensary. A charity health worker who bandaged wounds and, for a fee, handed out medicine and drugs, made irregular visits. The nearest hospital was 20 miles away and the bus passed by on the main road three times a week.

Ten per cent of the farmers owned 90 per cent of the land. They grew rice, castor for cooking oil, sunflowers, maize and various wheats, red, black and green gram (lentils and pulses), some tobacco and cotton. Mango and papaya trees grew here, and among the live-stock maintained were oxen, buffaloes, cows, sheep, goats, pigs and chickens. One farmer owned a diesel-operated tractor and everyone else tilled the land using an ox-drawn wooden plough.

In the main, the inhabitants of Cheemalkondor conducted their lives in a peaceful and harmonious manner. No one recollected any serious crime being committed within the community, and petty offences were dealt with by the panchayat, which was elected from the upper castes. The only recent disaster to afflict the community was the failure of the monsoon rains one year, when much of the livestock perished. The following harvest was a mere tenth of the normal yield, causing widespread hardship and misery. Little had changed in terms of social progress since my visit some five years previously, but the postman who had welcomed me many times in his home had lost a great deal of weight and his hair was now almost completely white. He had five daughters and only one son, and in order to raise money for the girls' dowries he had had to sell off most of his land and now was worrying over how he would be able to pay to have his son decently educated. However, he seemed delighted to see me and to meet my son and together we sat down and discussed which would be a suitable family to interview.

In the villages around the periphery of Hyderabad tie-and-dye weaving is a way of life. It is called ikat and is a traditional, inherited skill that has prospered in today's commercial world. In Cheemalkondor many families' lives revolve around the different aspects of weaving. The woven silk threads, dyed in many colours, are everywhere laid out to dry in the narrow streets. The craftsmen belonged to the Sudra caste and I thought it would be interesting to talk to a family at the heart of village life who had been associated with ikat for many generations, but who, through twentieth-century technology, could foresee a change in their situation. At this stage of my research I was interested in talking to people who had some command over their economic status and control over their destiny, people who maybe owned some land and who weren't entirely caught up in the struggle of simply surviving – people who were in touch with some of the changes taking place in the rest of the country.

Thirty-five-year-old weaver Kistaih Dashratha and his brother Kasturi, eleven years younger, resided together with their parents, wives and children on the same plot where their ancestors had lived for many generations. Their father Istari was still head of the household, although he was now retired. Kistaih was married to Pushpa and had three surviving children, and Kasturi and his young wife, Padma, had two. They were aware of the need to reduce their families but, infant mortality still being high, to stop at two was considered a risk. I found them warm and intelligent and each time we met they were as curious about my life in a European city as I was about theirs in the Indian countryside.

When I began to write this book I was surprised how ignorant many people in the cities were of rural life and of the people who inhabited the villages. On one occasion, six months after my first meeting with the Dashratha family, I asked the wife of a professor of social science at the technical college in Hyderabad if she would accompany me to Cheemalkondor on one of my visits to act as my interpreter and talk to the women.

'Why do you want to go to a village? Only stupid people live there,' she scoffed. The remark left me tongue-tied, but she agreed to come. I told her that if we went to the market before our departure, we could purchase a chicken and vegetables and fruits which were not readily available outside the city. Our hosts would prepare the food for us and themselves. We should just take our own water. The following morning when she came to pick me up there was a large picnic hamper on the back seat of her car. She was happy for me to purchase food as a gift but we should eat the food her mother had prepared for us. I was wearing a simple shirt and loose trousers, she a brightly coloured and fashionably designed silk chiffon salwar-kameez outfit – the Punjabi traditional dress so popular in all the cities. Whereas I wanted to keep as low a profile as possible, in an effort to encourage the womenfolk to relax and confide in us, she was determined that she was going to be a dazzling visitor.

When we arrived at the Dashrathas' home we were greeted with the warmth and hospitality so prevalent in rural India. My interpreter found herself unexpectedly drawn into intimate discussion with the brothers, both she and they curious to find out more about the other.

'It is only economics which makes your life different from ours,' Kasturi pointed out. We concurred, and proceeded after all to eat the food our hosts prepared for us in their kitchen, while their children consumed the Hyderabadi delicacies. After a few hours my interpreter, now converted to believing that wise and intelligent people also lived outside Hyderabad, set off home, leaving me behind with my notebook, cameras, tape recorder and sleeping bag.

All the family slept on rush mats without pillows. Mosquitoes abounded through the rainy season but they believed they had built up an immunity to them and slept without nets. In the hottest months they left all the doors open to allow any welcome breeze to blow through the house although the draught made the looms creak and groan in the night.

On the February night I stayed there, while the other inhabitants of Cheemalkondor slept, lights shone late into the evening in the Dashratha household. Istari's son-in-law, a tailor from the small neighbouring town of Bhongir, had come to stay bringing the gift of a plucked chicken. The meat was cut up and soaked in spices and a delicious meal prepared. Kasturi poured out the toddy and as the pungent alcohol loosened his tongue the young man began to give vent to his frustrations. He worked in partnership with his brother but the time had come when he wanted to see some reward for his labours. He wanted to keep what he earned for himself and his own family, instead of supporting the family of his elder brother, Kistaih, and his parents. Cries and shouts of arguing could be heard in the still calm of the night.

'This joint family effort is a load of old carbuncles. You never work properly and the way you idle away your time just holds me back,' Kasturi yelled at his brother.

'What's the matter with you, you crazy bastard?' retorted Kistaih.

'So if I'm a bastard, what does that make you? You can't have been born to the same mother as me. You're just the son of some whore our father picked up.'

'Come on, show a bit of respect. You don't seem to have it for anyone now. You even ignore your own sister when she comes to visit. Anyway, you can't talk to me about not working, the way you loaf around sometimes.'

Unaccustomed to the effects of strong liquor, Kasturi continued to shout incoherent abuse, unable to conduct a logical argument.

'Oh go on, fuck your own mother if you can't make it with your own wife any more. Anyway my sister only comes to see you. She can't stand the sight of me and I certainly don't want to see her so why should I have to feed her and her little brats?'

Loath to retire while their husbands brawled, the young wives were sitting by the looms, silently working on the silk frames, their small children asleep by their feet. Neither of them would consider entering the argument but, whatever the outcome, each would support her own husband, ignoring her personal opinion on the matter.

'Look,' suggested Kasturi. 'Why don't we divide the house in two, then I can just feed my own family as I have fewer children than you. I'll put forward this plan to the panchayat. I'll get my way, you'll see.'

'And what about our parents? Who will look after them?'

'Well, one month they can stay with me and one month they can stay with you.'

'Okay,' agreed Kistaih. 'That's not a bad idea at all. But let's go about it peacefully. No more rows or beatings. Let's put an end to losing our tempers and stop hitting out at each other. Remember, too, that we're both equal, both our needs are the same, so there's no need to be in a hurry. Come on, father, what's your opinion of this?'

'Oh for heaven's sake, I've had enough of your arguments. I'm reaching my end now, so you can make all the decisions. I'll just get on with whatever work I am able to do, and eat and sleep. I don't want to touch problems any more.' Their sixty-year-old father started to yawn, laid a large sheet on the floor and stretched out. There was nothing more to be said.

The following morning the two brothers rose late, after the effects of the alcohol had passed. Long before they had woken up, their wives had been cleaning around the sleeping men. Kistaih's wife, Pushpa, had sketched a flowered pattern with powdered rice at the bottom of the steps outside their front door, a welcome to the gods to bless the home and purge it of the ill-feelings expressed the previous evening.

'These rows are quite normal,' Kistaih confided to me. 'In fact they help to clear the air so I don't mind. When there are problems we have to talk about them. Living so close to each other as we do, how can we keep secrets from each other? Bad feeling can make life intolerable. I'm not really bothered by Kasturi's language. His personality is not suited to the repetition of loom work and I can see how frustrated he gets. It's easier for me because I know what makes me happy. It's quite simple. Water in the well, good and flourishing crops. Our land can be so hard and unyielding so what a pleasure it is when the earth is soft and pliable and one sees abundant growth in the fields. What a joy!'

On the other hand, Kasturi was treated with caution within the community. Everyone knew he was constantly on the lookout for ways and means of expanding his business, always scheming and operating and suspicious of any visitor and trader, and quick to recognise similar traits of personality in others, whereas the friendly yet hardworking Kistaih was universally liked and admired.

Their late grandfather was held in great respect in the village having taught himself the background and methods of ayurvedic medicine. The term ayurveda originated from ayus, meaning life, and veda, meaning knowledge of science. The theory operates on the principle that the body is made up of certain temperaments which must be kept in balance. The body has to be made strong enough to resist disease, so if someone falls ill one doesn't attempt to find a cure but tries to restore the equilibrium of the body through adjusting the diet. It is a philosophical system, a knowledge of life, but although its cures have been practised for centuries, the original theories were for much of that time distorted and only within the last hundred years has the practice gained more positive acceptance. The old man passed on his acquired knowledge to his eldest son and with the money the son made from his patients he purchased land, over 50 acres, which he shared with his brother Istari. Istari, as the youngest son, was taught the traditional family skill of weaving. However, after thirty years on the loom, he happily conceded his place to *his* younger son when Kasturi finished school. Physically the work looked easy going but prolonged sessions sitting down put great strain on the knee joints.

'Now I can take my time in the morning with my toilet, washing and dressing. At my leisure I can think about God and set up my own little puja table. I believe in a balanced combination of action and prayer.' He even announced that he was preparing himself for death. 'Well I keep changing my mind about living for a long time. I'm ready for the end now, it can happen any time.'

'So, go on then. What are you waiting for?' his wife joked, bursting into laughter.

'How do I know when I'm going to die, you stupid woman?' he retorted. 'All I say is that it's better just to be ready for it. Look,' he continued, 'every decent man in India considers it his duty to see that his children are married and that his sons have good wives. My daughters are married, my sons are married, my daughters-in-law are fine girls and have produced good sons, so what need is there for me to go on living? I don't think I have the energy to cope with any more problems, so maybe while I am content within myself this would be a good time to say farewell to this life.'

Istari, however, was in fine health and would still walk to the fields and do a little hoeing; his wife, only five years his junior, regularly worked eight hours a day, weeding and sowing, when there was the need. His sons loyally conceded that he was still head of the family even though he was no longer capable of making decisions, did little of practical use and had to be looked after, clothed and fed.

'I remember when, some twenty years ago, special medical camps were held locally offering vasectomies in exchange for a sack of grain or seed. People living here are cautious of a new venture but I've always been a renegade and I was the first man in this village to volunteer for the operation. Now look how strong I am today. I've had smallpox and cholera too, but, as you can see, I'm a survivor. My sons are always complaining but they don't seem to realise how much better things are for them nowadays and how much more prosperous they are generally. I used to work much harder than they do and, even taking into account inflation, I never made as much as they do now. Nor are they plagued by the deadly diseases which attacked us.' But he took great delight in watching his sons prosper, feeling a surge of pride when they dressed up in smart Western-style trousers and shirts to visit Hyderabad.

'I don't have a favourite son but even if I did I wouldn't say. It's not because I'm a diplomat. It's just in my interest to keep quiet about such matters because the least favoured son might poison my food!'

There were twenty families of weavers in Cheemalkondor, all directly or indirectly related to one another, and there was plenty of interaction and socialising between them and the other families. Most of the weavers helped each other out in small ways, lending thread and dyes and the like. However, they adopted a tougher attitude when someone went through a particularly difficult patch. Although goodwill was the intention, everyone fought for himself and was careful with his generosity – bad times were not unusual for anybody.

The Dashrathas' whitewashed house was light and spacious. Two looms filled up half of the living room, which led directly on to the street. There was a central gap in the clay-tiled roof which enabled them to work by daylight until the early evening. The family had more privacy than most of their neighbours, Kasturi and Kistaih having separate bedrooms which they shared with their wives and younger children. The older children slept in the living room with their grandparents. Their simple furnishings consisted of one small table, a carved wooden bench with its arm-rests missing and three upright wooden armchairs.

They had their own fresh-water well at the back of the house which was about 40 feet deep. When the supply was plentiful they happily allowed their neighbours to help themselves. However, despite living close to the Harijan community they only allowed them to draw water in a dire emergency and even then would insist that they took the pot and filled it up for them.

The kitchen, about 10 feet square, was detached from the back of the house. There were two clay open fires, one for wood, which produced a strong flame, and one for cow dung, which gave a gentler heat for simmering. Occasionally they had to purchase wood but they preferred to cut it from the trees on their own land. There was little ventilation from the small windows and the ceiling rafters were coated with smoke stains.

There was no drainage system in the village, only ten houses having any form of water closet. Behind the well they had a small latrine but there was no hole, just a tin door to allow a little privacy. Urine was absorbed into the ground, some running into their neighbour's courtyard where it irrigated some tomato and cucumber plants. Normally they relieved themselves in the open fields.

Fourteen years earlier they paid 150 rupees to have their home connected to the recently installed local supply of electricity. Although they were initially bewildered by such a modern amenity it seemed a practical option because they could then continue to weave when the sun went down. A year later they purchased a radio, and some of their neighbours had even started to cook on a small electric ring.

To relax, Kasturi sat in the house smoking cigarettes or bidis, while the philosophical Kistaih liked to go for an evening stroll or take the twenty-minute walk to look at the family acreage, where he also enjoyed working on the soil, weeding and threshing. He was happy in his own company and as the elder son he needed to work out in his own mind how to cope with his increasing responsibilities. Once he went to Pune and Bombay where he spent a week but he didn't like it. 'There were far too many people. Every room was crammed with bodies. Here I have air and space.' Kasturi, on the other hand, contemplated going to live in Hyderabad. He was restless and bored by the monotony and limitations of life in the village.

Girls rarely inherit land although often it has to be sold to raise money for their dowries. The 26 acres owned by Istari Dashratha would pass to Kistaih and Kasturi after his death. To till the soil and raise the crops they employed three labourers from the community of Shepherds, a Sudra subcaste. They would never consider giving employment to a Harijan. In lieu of payment the workers received a half-share of the harvest.

'When we have surplus crops we hire a bullock and cart to take the goods to market at Bhongir, ten miles from here,' Kasturi explained. It cost 30 rupees to hire the cart and they would set off with the load as the sun rose around six in the morning, arriving at twelve noon. If, when they had covered their travelling costs and purchased a few household essentials, there were some rupees to spare from the sale of their stock, they went straight to the cooperative bank to purchase sacks of fertiliser – 'Senseless to return to Cheemalkondor with an empty bullock cart.'

Kasturi's brother-in-law was a tailor working in Bhongir and he made the family's shirts. 'He's quite cunning and we have to pay him although he says he gives us a special price. Fifteen rupees for his labour for one shirt and twelve rupees for the cotton material and he says he charges his other customers a total of thirty-five rupees.'

When I first visited the Dashrathas their acreage was flourishing at the start of the monsoon. Kistaih was characteristically optimistic that there was plenty more rain on the way. He was to be disappointed. The few meagre showers which ensued were barely enough to water the summer crop let alone fill the well for the winter harvest. Five months later, he disconsolately wandered over the fields. The second crop which should have been ready for harvesting well in time for the Sankranti harvest festival was reduced to a few dried-out stalks. They had heard rumours that the government had plans to bore wells where the water shortage was most severe but they were sceptical. Few such promises are ever carried out and they had already decided to abandon sowing seed for that winter and wait for the next year's rains.

By half-past seven every morning, Kistaih and Kasturi were seated at their looms. They worked for about three hours, during which time they could each complete one yard of cloth. Then they took a late breakfast, their children having already been fed and the elder ones despatched to school. Afterwards they worked for three more hours, before lunch in the mid-afternoon, followed by a short rest. They did a further two hours' work in the evening. Dinner was at eight and they settled down for the night at half-past nine.

Between them Kistaih and Kasturi usually completed fifteen saris every month, following a local pattern. Up to four different colours were used in each sari, including glorious pinks, greens, mauves, scarlets and white, each dramatic combination standing out boldly in contrast with the simplicity of their whitewashed home.

They were an efficient team, slowly and silently working around each other. The art of tying rubbers to lay out the design with its many motifs, including the shape of an elephant, was very complicated, but as the children were always playing around the looms and watching their parents work, by the time they were old and strong enough to handle a loom they had fully acquired the expertise. Padma and Pushpa helped the men boil and spin the silk, and then thread it on to a wooden frame known as a shank and fix the rubbers prior to the dyeing process. Pushpa was so deft and swift she could do it while she was breastfeeding. Both girls had married in their early teens, and neither had thought much about her individual

101

desires. They were absorbed into the economic structure, aware that if they worked hard they would all prosper together.

Only Kistaih and Kasturi worked on the looms, standing inside a large trough dug into the floor, a more comfortable position than the traditional one of sitting cross-legged. The looms were constructed by their grandfather over fifty years ago, and the mechanics had not changed since their conception 1,500 years ago. There were five thousand threads in the width of each sari and nearly fifteen thousand in the length, and the weaver had to stop briefly each time a skein of silk was fed through to make sure the pattern was correctly aligned.

Each completed garment was sold directly to a main dealer for 380 rupees and a customer in a store would pay 500 rupees for it. Three hundred rupees was spent on raw materials for each sari which included silk, dye and rubber strips. Two whole days were spent designing and dyeing the thread and one sari then took four days to weave. Thus they each earned approximately 15 rupees daily, 50 per cent more than an agricultural labourer. Every month Kistaih and Kasturi took the bus to Hyderabad to purchase silk yarn and dyes, spending about 3,000 rupees a trip. They did not have a current account at a bank so they kept their money locked up in an old tin trunk in the back store room.

'Everything that is earned is put into the same box,' explained their father. 'We take it as we need it. Despite my younger son's frustrations, we still maintain a sense of mutual trust. If there is a shortage we all know that it is the children who will suffer.'

Kistaih was thankful to have inherited a skill and trade which enabled him to keep body and soul together but Kasturi was always interested in other ways of increasing their income. Deciding to capitalise on the electricity connection they have in their home, he purchased a motorised chilli-grinder in Hyderabad. He had to bring it to the village in the back of a truck, the engine and steel pounders being so heavy. With bribes and transport it cost them 6,000 rupees but grinding dried chilli to a fine powder by hand is a laborious task and most people would happily forgo a few rupees to let a machine do the work. Already it was earning them 300 rupees a month. Including the interest owed on the purchase loan the machine would be completely paid for in two years. Then it would be profit all the way.

Throughout the whole of the country, within the weavers' communities there is a paradox. The level of inflation is continually escalating, so that many skilled hand-weavers have had to seek employment on power looms, where they can expect to earn more. Inevitably mechanisation has deprived millions of their livelihoods as cloth is produced more cheaply by fewer weavers, but now heavy excise duty on yarn supply to power looms is making them uneconomical too, so there are even more men without work. Mills are installing new automatic machinery so that the consumer can get better material at a lower cost. Eventually most handlooms will go out of business altogether. Although it is unlikely that the beautiful silk saris woven by the Dashrathas will ever be made on power looms, they are dependent on a diminishing market that is willing to pay a high price for quality. Adjustment to modern practices and the constant pressure of having to think of other means of survival has been a painful experience for the weavers. There is a very high level of sophistication in weaving going back thousands of years, and it will be a tragedy when this skill and knowledge becomes unviable. Handloom weavers are the second largest trained workforce in India and there are still ten million of them working today.

Kistaih and his wife were still mourning the loss of their second son, Pandari. He was only eight years old when he died. He and his school friends had spent a morning in May fooling around and splashing each other with the cold water from a local well. They dried themselves off in the burning midsummer sun. That night he was violently sick and developed a high fever which raged for about ten days. His mother sat with him all the time. Finally his temperature started to drop and he began sleeping a lot. As he calmed down he seemed to be over the worst but one morning he woke early and started to vomit again. While she held him in her arms, gently rocking his shaking body, he stopped breathing. Kistaih could not rid himself of a deep feeling of sadness whenever the boy's name was mentioned. To console himself he had erected a small shrine in his memory in a corner of the store room and he kept a small oil lamp with its flame continually alight.

Although the children of the family mixed with Harijans in the classroom, they rarely played with them after school and never invited them into their home, as their grandfather, like many others in his community, was quite contemptuous of the Untouchables. 'I have given it a lot of thought. Of course, I do have a desire to do well towards my neighbour, but these fellows – even if they're not actually different from us, their habits certainly are. They don't wash themselves properly and their attitudes are quite slovenly. I've watched how the government keeps on giving them more and more incentives but they just drink it all away.' Although he lived less than 50 yards from their dwellings, he overlooked the simple practical difficulties imposed by their primitive water facilities and cramped living conditions. The small wage they received barely covered the cost of their food let alone allowed them to dress decently and keep their children clean.

Every year, prior to Diwali, Istari asked the dhobi to whitewash the interior of their house which was then decorated with garlands of leaves from the mango tree. On the first day of the festival they made a special puja to Lakshmi and gave offerings of specially prepared sweets to the other gods. On the second day relatives were invited to stay and a small feast was prepared. On the third day, when the relatives departed they were presented with gifts of clothing. Although the girls never wore the saris their husbands wove, they enjoyed dressing up and still wore their wedding saris at festival time.

For four decades life in Cheemalkondor had continued peacefully and little had disturbed the rhythm of the working day and the unfolding of each year, marked by a ritual of traditional festivities and the anticipation of a good or poor monsoon. However, during the drought that I witnessed, the Dashrathas lost all their livestock including ten beautiful Jersey cows. They were devastated. 'The cow is like our second mother, a member of the family who lives in our hearts. When all of ours died it wasn't just the absence of milk which hurt us, but their presence as part of the family which we grieved,' they explained. It was a blow to their confidence in their ability to take care of animals, too, so the herd was never replaced. The theft of the family's gold jewellery, valued at over 7,000 rupees, added

21 The Dashratha family   22, 23 & 24 Pushpa and Padma husk gram, grind chilli on their husbands' machine, and pound millet   25 Kistaih threads up the warp of a sari   26 Padma prepares yarn for the weft

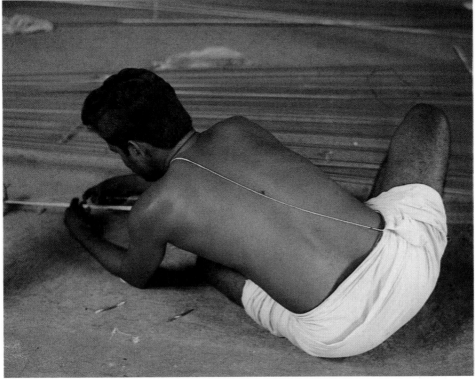

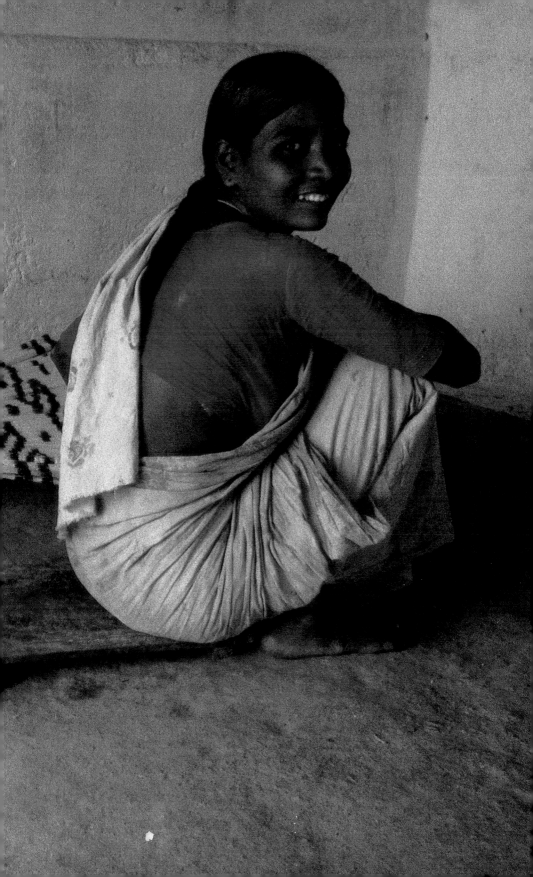

to the trauma at this time. During the marriage ceremony of Istari's elder daughter, a young man ran up to the bride and wrenched it all off her neck. The culprit was never caught or identified.

Neither Kistaih nor Kasturi had any knowledge of the history of the area or the village but Istari still remembered from his childhood tales told of Kazim Razvi, a Muslim with violent ideals who was anti-British, anti the governing body in Hyderabad led by the princely family of the Nizams, who were also Muslims, and opposed to the proposed terms of a united India.

'The British were never here in the true sense although, just before the days of the Raj ended, their troops visited this village.' Prior to 1947, Hyderabad was an independent state governed by the Nizams. It had its own army, currency, postal and broadcasting systems and railway network. The Nizam at the time wavered under the threat of a divided country, whereby Pakistan would be created and Hyderabad would be absorbed by the Hindus. Kazim emerged as a rival during this period of indecision, rising with a Nazi-like fanaticism from among the impoverished section of Muslims. In 1947 Hyderabad declared that it would remain an independent state and even dispatched its own ambassador to London. Meanwhile Kazim Razvi and his men were on a witch hunt.

'Word of Communism began reaching us,' remembered Istari, 'but to show any interest was a considerable hazard as Razvi's men seemed hell-bent on destroying any interest in such ideals. Woe unto any Hindu with Communist sympathies. There was quite a lot of agitation around here, even in the village. Whole families were taken from their homes and immediately shot. Many had their homes raided and money and support were forcibly extorted. In fear most of us conceded, but we had no idea really what we were conceding to. The Muslims suspected every Hindu of being a Communist. I saw the poorer people in the village suffering the most. Uninformed and unarmed they were most vulnerable to harassment.' Razvi's 'Razakar' movement penetrated deep into the countryside with much greater effect than the Nizam's jurisdiction but on 13 September 1948 the whole state was captured and incorporated into a united India.

★

27 With her young son at her side, Padma unties rubber strips from the dyed silk   28 Pushpa and her husband Kistaih fold the newly-woven sari ready for delivery to the dealer in Hyderabad

Almost a year had elapsed since my first meeting with the Dashratha family. When we first met their land was flourishing and relations between Kasturi and Kistaih were tolerable despite the occasional turbulence. However, the miserable monsoon had reduced their crop yield to a third of its normal level and Kasturi had become more edgy and low-spirited. He also perceived the diminishing demand for their handwoven saris and was restless and eager to make a new start in Hyderabad, while still admitting the advantages of living in a joint family.

'If only there was a suitable opportunity, then nothing would stop me.'

His father thought he was crazy. 'Look,' he said. 'All of you would have to live in a room the size of our chicken coop and that would cost you at least three hundred rupees a month and on top of that you would have to pay for electricity. Why put yourself into a situation of inevitable deprivation?'

'No, you don't get the point,' argued Kasturi. 'I'll sell off my share of the land and involve myself in some business deal by using the capital. I'm sure I could make something work out.' He was adamant in his belief. There was much more on offer in the city – job opportunities, good education for his children, better training facilities and ultimately a better lifestyle. He would perhaps try his hand at trading in cloth. He wasn't daunted by the crowds and cramped living conditions.

'I go to Hyderabad once a month so I know what I'm talking about. I know how city life operates.' He looked at his elder brother who was grinning and shaking his head. 'So, it's a gamble, but the way I feel now I reckon it's one worth taking. It will be like a game of chess. If all goes well I will have check-mate but if it doesn't work out it's just too bad. Look at my father laughing. He thinks I want to go because of the movie houses, but he's wrong.'

Throughout his son's protestation, Istari sat seemingly impassive. Occasionally a smile passed across his heavily pock-marked face. He knew that while he was still alive Kasturi couldn't sell any land. His lad was just boasting and dreaming. But he kept his thoughts to himself. All of them needed a fantasy sometimes. The last time I saw him he took me to one side and told how he was going to sort out his sons' differences. 'This constant arguing is too much for all of us and I consider it my responsibility to put a stop to it.' He took me by the elbow and led me to the back door.

'We will build another house. Our plot of land extends to beyond the kitchen and there is just enough room. I have two sons, so there must be one house and one loom for each. There's a stone quarry some two miles from here and we can use the wood from the neem tree to carve the frames for the doorways and make the beams. We will all build it together but I am not moving from here. I built this house with my father so that's one good reason for staying put. When the new house is complete Kistaih and Kasturi can decide for themselves who will live there.'

6

A Brahmin Family in Tamil Nadu

The most orthodox Brahmins live in South India and when preparing to find a suitable family I felt apprehensive. As a European, I believed that I would be unlikely to be welcomed into a priest's home for fear of polluting the premises, so I decided to enlist the help of a Christian friend who ran a small health clinic 40 miles south of Madras. Her practice was not far from one of the largest temples in the neighbourhood, in a small town overlooking the Bay of Bengal in Tamil Nuda. As the only doctor in the area I anticipated that she would be on familiar terms with most of the inhabitants.

'You won't find it easy,' she warned me. 'These people are wary of outsiders and they only come to me in desperation when one of their children is really sick. As soon as the child is cured, they often ignore me.' Although she was not encouraging, she took me to the house of the chief custodian of the local temple. The only person at home was his wife. Everyone else had gone away for the day on a pilgrimage to a shrine some 50 miles away. In the far corner of the darkened room I could make out the shape of a middle-aged lady lying on the floor. When she saw us she got up and smiled but she didn't move towards us. She had been left behind because she had her period and for three days would eat and sit alone. She suggested we went to the house of Doraiswamy Battacharia. He was a custodian in the same temple as her husband

and lived opposite. We crossed the main square to where she had indicated.

In the doorway I could see an old man crouched down, turning the pages of a well-thumbed book. Apart from a string of beads hanging around his neck and a knee-length cotton dhoti which was tied about his waist, he was naked. His head was shaved except for one long white knotted tuft at the back. As I approached I could see that he was reading a horoscope for a client, consulting the position of the stars to see what would be a suitable name for the man's ten-day-old son. We waited until they had finished. From inside I could hear the high-pitched voice of an old woman.

'Don't talk to her,' she screeched. 'She's a spy working for the government.' I lingered cautiously by the door until the commotion inside abated. A man of about forty came out, the old man's son. He was similarly dressed except that his hair ran wild and long down his shoulders. We smiled at each other and I explained the reason for my visit, resolving that I would probably have to make do by conducting my discussions on their doorstep. But soon I felt inhibited by the curiosity of the neighbours who crowded around to watch and listen and I asked if I could step inside. I was told to come back the following morning, when they had had time to think over my proposals, and I returned to my friend's home in a mood of pessimism.

I wondered how I could persuade them to talk to me and convince them that they would not be threatened by my enquiries. Later that evening we had a visit from the gentleman who was having his new-born son's horoscope read. His name was Dhamo and he worked as a guide in English for the tourists who visited the temple. He told me that Doraiswamy had a granddaughter of twenty-three and the family were desperate to find a husband for her. They had fallen on hard times of late and were unable to raise a sufficient dowry. If they talked to me, maybe I could make a contribution. I hesitated. I didn't want to do anything that would signify my approval of a system which I regarded as abhorrent. I would be happy to give the family some rupees for the time I spent with them, time which would take them from their priestly duties, and instead of money maybe I could donate some gifts in anticipation of a wedding, some household goods and saris.

The following day Dhamo took me back to Doraiswamy's house and to my surprise and relief I was invited in. This first meeting was quite straightforward. Everyone was at home, eager to meet the foreigner. I took photographs including polaroid snaps which I gave them to keep. Giving them instant prints had the desired effect of gaining their confidence and soon they began answering my questions without much hesitation.

Doraiswamy, a Vishnavite priest and a devotee of Vishnu, the preserver of life, was nearly eighty years old. Despite his advanced years and emaciated frame, he was still a strong man in basically good health, his eyes bright and shining. His wife, Kamala, fifteen years younger than him, was in a much more frail condition. She was physically disabled, her legs twisted and bowed, although she could still walk to the latrine, or to the well to wash, with the aid of a stick. Most of the time she sat hunched up on the floor, squatting beside her husband's feet. They shared their home with two of their children and their young families. There was their son Srinivasa, aged forty-five, his wife of thirty-five, Rajalakshmi, and their five children, and their daughter Premamani (the second of four) and her husband, Krishnaswami, with four surviving children – in all, fifteen members and three generations of one family living together under one roof.

Srinivasa was a priest working in the same temple as his father, and his own eldest son, Ravi, was there too, doing his apprenticeship under the tutelage of his grandfather. Srinivasa's wife was a second cousin whom he married when she was only thirteen years old. Ravi's brother Anand, who at sixteen was four years the junior, dreamt of becoming a doctor, an unusual choice of profession for the son of a priest.

'What lofty ideas he has,' confined Srinivasa. 'I won't say he's not bright enough. That wouldn't be fair. But he would rather play with his friends than spend time with a book. Suresh [the youngest at twelve] is the brightest of my sons and he could go far. Maybe one day he will join me in the temple and take Ravi's place for he doesn't have a true calling for the work. It's really something to keep him occupied because he doesn't seem to have any other particular ambition.'

Both the younger boys were still studying at the local government school with their two sisters, Sujatha, who was nine, and Anuradha, six.

'We don't know how the girls will develop, but we think they're growing up well,' said their parents. They would not be encouraged to seek employment, but their father wanted them to have just sufficient education so that they could read and write efficiently.

Although they were closely related, Srinivasa first met Rajalakshmi on their wedding day. 'The early years of our marriage was a good time, just one child and not too many responsibilities. But she has taken a large family in her stride and she's very attached to the children. In fact she's devoted to them, and to me too. I'm a lucky man!'

Some five years ago a government family welfare clinic visiting their town distributed information regarding a sterilisation programme for women. With five children already, the idea appealed to Rajalakshmi and she proceeded with the small operation, regarding the 100 rupees she had to pay as a wise investment.

Premamani had two daughters and two sons ranging in age from six to twenty-one. It was unusual to find among their peers a grown daughter and her family living with her parents. When Premamani got married she went to live with her husband's family. They were custodians of a temple in an area 30 miles inland where, owing to years of excessive extremes of drought and flooding, great rural poverty prevailed. Maintaining the livelihoods of the priests there, was a low priority and the temple building was on the verge of collapse. With a large family to feed, Krishnaswami had no other option but to turn for help to his father-in-law. As the old man's health was a little frail at the time, he decided to apportion some of his workload to Krishnaswami and made room for them all in his own home.

Despite their lean frames, the whole family was extremely fit, and for generations most of their forefathers had lived to a good old age. They had never practised any form of meditation, believing that prayer was sufficient. Srinivasa attributed their good health to a combination of vegetarian diet and abstention from alcohol and tobacco, which they believed to be the most polluting of substances. Cycling as much as 16 miles a day in the course of carrying out all the priestly duties was an exercise which kept their limbs strong and supple.

Yet general ignorance still took its toll. Last summer Premamani and her husband lost a twelve-year-old son who lay sick for two days with a bad attack of diarrhoea before slipping away in his mother's arms late in the evening of the second day.

'We don't want to think about him. If we do we all start to cry. We simply cremated his body and threw the ashes into the sea.'

My doctor friend later told me that she could have saved the boy if they had consulted her. 'When a child has bad trouble with its stomach, they think he has a pox of the intestines. These families blame the gods for the illness, believing it to be some form of punishment for a misdeed. If they consult a doctor and give the child some medicine they think the gods will be annoyed. Instead they take a leaf from the neem tree and some saffron and prepare a mixture and then just offer it in prayer, rubbing the child's body with handfuls of the potion. Unfortunately this boy died from medical negligence. He was suffering from acute amoebic dysentery. As a result of a lack of water passing through his gut the infection perforated the intestine, causing multiple ulcers and internal bleeding. He died of dehydration. If I had seen him I would have given him drugs and fed him orally with glucose. I see so many people dying here because they see disease as a sign of the gods avenging themselves. They die of measles, elephantiasis, malaria, cholera. All are regarded as the pox, and yet I can cure them all.'

Economics also discouraged them from spending their meagre earnings on medical help if they thought they could cure an illness with a herb growing in their yard. It was their impoverished state which had so far prevented Krishnaswami and Premamani finding a suitable husband for their eldest daughter, Jayanti, despite her easy-going personality and fine-featured face with its warm and ready smile.

'I don't mind making a contribution, giving the bride some clothes and cooking pots, these things are all right,' her father told me, 'but ten thousand rupees is the minimum we will have to raise. She will need a silk sari, food for the wedding feast, some jewellery and gifts for her husband's family. How can we raise this I wonder?' He looked at me as though expecting I would interrupt him with a gesture of compliance but I stayed silent waiting for him to continue.

'We have nothing at all saved. Soon she will be too old. I have heard there is a law against dowries, but it is never enforced. If it were, I should be an extremely happy man.' At this I nodded my head in agreement.

The Brahmin procedures for finding a suitable husband were similar to the customs adopted by other Hindu communities and, though the family themselves socialised little, temple work facilitated introductions amongst the Vishnavite Brahmins. Once a prospective husband was found the parents would suggest how much they could afford, and then it would be up to the boy's family to decide if the sum was sufficient. The price would be high if the young man had a good job, or prospects of working for the government or in a bank.

Although the question of a dowry for his granddaughter caused anxiety, Doraiswamy believed absolutely in arranged marriages. 'Only such unions have sound and healthy roots. As temple life is very sociable, suitable unions within our own communities of Brahmins are, on the whole, easy for us to arrange,' he explained to me. When I asked him if divorce could ever be tolerated within their community he rolled his eyes in horror – such an action would present the worst kind of threat to economic and religious stability. However, there was evidence that the temptation was there not to concur with family wishes in other respects. A combination of education and the need to earn more, simply to survive, placed pressure on many of Doraiswamy's colleagues to find a vocation outside the temple.

Doraiswamy's eldest daughter died when she was fifteen years old. She fell into the temple tank and drowned – 'A lovely girl but maybe she was too good for this life and the gods decided to call her to them early.' The fourth daughter married for love and, despite her husband being from their own community, the Battacharias condemned the match and cut themselves off from all contact with her.

I looked down at my notebook, realising that there was one more daughter. Doraiswamy anticipated my next question and clasped his hands together. 'The gods were angry and they punished her,' he said, looking me straight in the eye. I hesitated, and from his glare

thought best at this moment to change the subject. In fact, I felt that
our discussion had reached a conclusion for the first day – a good
introduction had been made with enough ground covered – and I got
up from the floor, touching my forehead in a gesture of gratitude and
thanks. As we walked back to the doctor's house Dhamo told me the
story.

'Much to the surprise and horror of her family, Doraiswamy's third
daughter eloped when she was eighteen years old with a young boy
who was working as a waiter in a local restaurant. They met in the
baker's shop where he worked in the mornings. Shortly after her
father discovered the affair the couple left the town and settled in
Madras, so that they knew little about the boy's background except
for his origins in the Naicker community [of the Banya or business
caste]. The girl's departure left her father feeling deeply ashamed
and angry. For quite some time he could not bear to show his
face in public, and he took to his bed for nearly two months,
even shunning his duties in the temple. When news of her death
reached him, Doraiswamy was delighted. Rumour had it that she had
haemorrhaged after attempting to abort her unborn child.' I realised
from this sad tale that I had met a family whose whole approach to
life was completely different from my own and if they were going to
continue talking to me I would have to tread very carefully indeed.

The temple where Doraiswamy and his son worked was situated
in a small sea port of some six thousand inhabitants. The main catch
of the local fishermen consisted of lobsters, prawns and small sharks.
The town was regularly visited by people making a pilgrimage to
its large Hindu temple, and from this a major industry had evolved
– the carving and selling of granite statues of gods and goddesses.
From dawn to dusk the air was filled with the noise of the hard rock
being cut and chiselled in stonemasons' yards situated throughout the
town's backstreets. Stonemasonry was a relatively modern skill in
India and the craftsmen, who came from all castes, were beginning to
break down social barriers in the traditionally caste-ridden society.

Unlike the lush western coastal region of Kerala, a strip of
mountainous tropical land blessed with rich soil producing an
abundance of tea, coffee, pepper, pineapples and other exotic fruits,
the south-eastern state of Tamil Nadu is flat and sparse. There is the

occasional relief of mango groves and tall coconut trees, but otherwise the Tamils have to toil hard to cultivate their paddy, water melons and ragi (a variety of mustard seed), and their orchards of cashews and peanuts. Salt is collected from fields flooded by the exceptionally high tide. Small wonder that two centuries ago, worn out by their unyielding lands, farmers took their families across the water to the island of Sri Lanka, a small haven of uncultivated forest and verdant fertility.

Along the coast, circular three-storey concrete edifices, constructed by the government to provide shelter during the cyclones and heavy rains so prevalent in the area, had been converted into temporary camps for Tamil refugees driven back from the lands their forefathers tilled and seas they fished by small groups of Sri Lankans, Buddhists and nationalist fanatics.

Despite their proximity to the ocean, Srinivasa said he had never learnt to swim. 'I'm really frightened by the very rough sea on this coastline, and it's deceptive too. It dips very suddenly and there are massive jagged rocks very close to the shore. Nothing would persuade me even to go out in a boat there!

'Last year, shortly after my nephew passed away, we had the worst monsoon rains for – well, how long? – it must have been about fifteen years. It did not stop raining for ten days. The square outside was absolutely awash. Trees were uprooted and no transport could get through. The temple was completely flooded, so we were unable to carry out our normal duties.'

The fishermen suffered the most, many of them losing their boats, but being vegetarian Doraiswamy and his family were less affected until the crops were spoiled and the price of vegetables and rice rose steeply. Fortunately their house was built three steps above street level, making the foundations safe, but the roof was badly battered and they had to replace all the zinc sheeting when the rains finally stopped. It was two months before everything returned to normal.

Even in good years the climate was never easy. The summer months were invariably very hot. From the end of April until the middle of June the temperatures rarely fell below 40°C, and because of the proximity to the ocean the heat was accompanied by a cloying and uncomfortable humidity. In the winter months 24°C was the coolest weather normally experienced.

Although Doraiswamy showed a marked disinterest in contemporary activities in his town and state, he had good recall of local events during the Second World War.

'All the available food was sent to the army, but there was no fighting around here. I remember the soldiers pitching their tents on the outskirts of the town. It must have been some sort of military practice because they used to dig a big ditch and wear earphones and hide themselves, sending each other messages and moving around on all fours with bits of trees sticking out of their helmets. There were evacuees, too, brought from Madras, and even from the north of the country. I think they were shipped from Calcutta.

'As soon as it was dark we were forbidden to burn lamps. We were forced to sell most of the rice we grew, even if it was only just enough for ourselves. The authorities gave us very little money for it, but persuaded us it was our contribution to saving our country from evil forces. I never knew who those evil forces were exactly.'

I sensed that Doraiswamy enjoyed telling me about the past. Probably I was the first person he had talked to of these things for over forty years. He said he felt very nostalgic about the Raj. There was then no direct road connection to Madras but the British had built a canal at the beginning of the century. The local District Collector and traders came from the city by boat. There were British police stationed less than 10 miles away, but little crime was committed locally. Everyone would retire very early because there was no electricity. After six in the evening the whole town would just go to sleep. Even though the British built a road in 1943, the coastal road was not completed until as recently as 1962, and until then the temple was still used just by local inhabitants. Everything was good for the family in those days, which is something Doraiswamy doesn't feel today.

'There was general respect and honest dealings within the community, especially for us Brahmins. It's not the same any more. In my family, we lived our lives doing our duty and in the fear of God. All that has changed now. I confess it is the same even with myself. One is thinking so much about how much money one can get. It's this need which is corrupting society. I try to teach my grandchildren what is their moral duty but with outside influences it is an uphill task. I want them to cooperate with me but they don't. I tell them that if they act well they will receive goodness in this life and the next.'

His house was situated behind a row of shops in the centre of town. For generations his ancestors had lived there, though he had no knowledge of how and when it was originally acquired. It was a simple building with a large half-covered central courtyard.

For the adults, apart from temple and priestly duties, all their daily activities revolved around each other. Few visitors were allowed beyond the small entrance porch where Doraiswamy read horoscopes for his clients. For this purpose two stone benches had been built into the walls on either side.

'All transactions are carried out here. The barber comes, the vendors of milk and vegetables, and the electrician who comes to read the meter. Everyone can come, irrespective of caste and creed,' protested Srinivasa, yet in practice I noticed that the rest of his family were still wary and cautious of outsiders. They considered all people of other religions, Muslims and Christians, to be the same as the most backward of Hindus, Untouchables, but they kept their feelings to themselves, taking the utmost care not to incur hostility for fear of losing custom. When a Harijan was spotted hovering around the front entrance, or their back yard, they felt threatened and immediately put up the chain on the door, waiting until the 'trespasser' had passed by.

The old lady, Kamala, was exceptionally suspicious of any stranger attempting to come near her home, and should her husband suggest extending a little hospitality she would chide him. Continually, in my presence, she scolded Doraiswamy for talking to me. Sometimes either she or her grandchildren would peer out at visitors through a small crack in the heavy double doors which protected their home from the hurly-burly of life in the street, separating two totally different worlds. All through the day in the square outside there was a bustle of activity – cobblers, and vendors of coconut milk, fruit, sweets and all varieties of religious trinkets plied their wares; at the bus station many vehicles carried passengers to and fro between Madras and Pondicherry and offloaded devotees making a special pilgrimage to Doraiswamy's temple – while behind those thick doors

117

lived a Brahmin family who with every move, gesture and *modus vivendi* doggedly and tenaciously attempted to hold on to traditions from centuries past, the women rarely leaving the house. Their daily activities were confined to practicalities and their own religious rituals. They were an enclosed, compact unit of individuals reliant just on each other. They rarely entered into any discussion unless it was related to their religious duties or their economic problems. They showed neither interest nor curiosity about the world beyond their home and temple. Political discussion tended to give Srinivasa a headache. He was confused, and wondered why politicians should want to fight each other all the time. The family seemed afraid of the twentieth century, and the environment right outside their own home often frightened them. If there was trouble in the road – local shop-keepers squabbling among themselves or children throwing small stones at each other in jest – Srinivasa would bolt up the front door. Any hint of trouble and they simply did not wish to know.

The busy street seemed an unlikely setting for such a reclusive family. To the left, advertised in bold and bright letters, was the Aruna Radio House, offering sales and service for radio and television sets, and to the right was a photographer's shop, promising speedy development of colour and black-and-white prints. Both were once a part of the original homestead, but had been detached recently and let out for a modest sum of money to provide extra income. Srinivasa had rented a large black-and-white TV set from his tenant. As neither he nor his father was mechanically minded it had proved useful to have someone working at close quarters who could adjust their set and for this purpose they overlooked his belonging to an inferior caste and allowed him inside. The owner of the photo shop was from a subcaste of Brahmins, and so they were willing to allow him to extend his business and use one of their storage rooms as darkroom and studio.

On the ground floor of the house all the rooms opened on to the courtyard, which was an extension of the main room. When he was not working, Doraiswamy usually rested, seated in a reclining chair, while his wife squatted on a thin quilt laid out on the concrete floor. Many pictures of various incarnations of Krishna and his consorts, as well as a few family photographs, adorned the walls. The men had their puja shrine in one corner, around which were hung cheap framed prints of Vishnu, Rama, Lakshmi, Hanuman, and the goddesses Saraswathi and Sita, and a photograph of Doraiswamy's grandson Mohan, taken shortly after his death, with a red mark of blessing painted on to his forehead, hung alongside pictures of the gods. There was also a photograph of the daughter who drowned, a painting of the sacred cow marked with all the gods believed to pervade it, and a small wooden shelf on which were placed spare strands of the sacred thread.

Leading from the main room was another room where Doraiswamy and Kamala took their meals. Clothes were stored slung over the rafters. Three large tin trunks sat, one on top of the other, in a corner. They belonged to Kamala and she always kept them locked. She said the contents included clothes, bedding and personal jewellery but she was secretive about what else the trunks contained. A little light filtered in from a small glass pane fitted into the roof. In another corner there was a round iron stove – an old oil-can with holes punched in the side, turned upside down. On this they boiled water for tea and coffee over a small kerosene flame. Stored overhead on a wooden shelf were five aluminium cooking pots and twenty beakers used for drinking tea. Along one wall was an old bench, two tables and a chair piled high with pillows, though they ate their food squatting on the hard stone floor. Two threshing baskets hung on the badly stained walls. If they could afford it, they repainted them every other year. Doraiswamy kept his own oval eating dish and a round aluminium plate for Kamala stored under the table.

The tiny kitchen, about 5 feet square, adjoined a small dark room where they stored their cooking utensils and the women performed their puja. Pungent smoke stung the eyes as Rajalakshmi prepared the food on the two clay stoves, the only ventilation coming through a few broken tiles in the roof. Opposite the doorway there was a wooden bench on which were stacked four brass pots, about ten aluminium dishes, iron ladles blackened with grease and smoke, and an iron griddle for making chapattis.

Above the women's shrine were framed pictures including reproductions of the goddess Lakshmi, consort of Vishnu, and her incarnations, and the Lords Brahma and Shiva. There was a garlanded photograph of Rajalakshmi's mother who had died eight years previously, and on a sooty ledge they kept their offerings for their idols, boxes of the red cuncuman powder used for the tilaka mark, grated coconut and sandalwood, the holy thread used for a wick when they lit camphor, a small brass container, two plain white candles and little statues of various female idols.

The gods were invoked everywhere. Rangoli patterns, symbolising an invitation to the gods to visit the home, were painted on all available floor space, and on the stone seating. Hand-painted plaster of Paris figures of Ganesh and Hanuman, adorned with garlands of wilting buds of roses and dead heads of marigolds, were stuck over every door lintel.

Occasionally green lizards would crawl up the walls, hiding behind the picture-frames and inside the eaves of the roof. The family felt superstitious about their presence. Should one fall on someone's hair, there was a fight ahead, but if it landed on a shoulder good news was on the way. Small scorpions and flying beetles also nested in the tiles but insects of this nature were so common their presence went unnoticed.

Every Friday the women of the house fasted. They declined any food until after sunset and then took just a little rice with milk. In the morning, still wearing the saris which they kept on while they took their daily bath, they underwent an elaborate puja, the wet cotton clinging to their small frames, making many offerings to the gods with flowers, cow dung and sugar, while holding a small dish of burning camphor. Finally they knelt on the ground and kissed the mud floor with their lips, five times. When they were very young the children would pick up and learn these rituals. Often they sat close to their parents, with their eyes shut and their hands placed together, palm against palm. At ten years old they began to understand the meaning behind these prayers and to participate fully in the performance of puja.

Doraiswamy fasted every Saturday and on special religious days, an average of ten times a month.

A narrow stairway led from the courtyard to a small room where the children slept in the cooler months and a long roof terrace which overlooked the temple complex. Doraiswamy confessed that sometimes he could not stand the house. There were no windows, never a breeze. It was so dark, and in the hot months, even with the ceiling fan turned on, the atmosphere became extremely oppressive. Electricity cuts were frequent, too, especially during the night-time, and the air became quite stagnant.

'Just imagine it, so many of us living here. It's all right for the little ones – they can sleep on the open terrace – but the stairs are steep and narrow and there's no way either I or my wife can climb them. We have to stay down here and suffer.'

They owned a cow, a creature with the pretty features of the English Jersey. She wandered freely through the courtyard from the street outside to the garden at the rear. Purchased with the intention of providing them with milk, she was now expecting a calf, impregnated by an unknown bull on her daily wanderings around the town. Treated as a member of the family, she was affectionately called Vijaylakshmi – Viji for short. If a Harijan were ever to enter the house they would immediately catch the cow and wait for her to urinate so that they could sprinkle and purify the homestead when the hapless man had been expelled. Komiyum, cow's urine, was considered to be even holier and more pure than the water from their own well. The most heinous of crimes was to harm a cow. She was the true living incarnation of all the gods and to kill her would be a great sin. Such an act would result in the worst form of rebirth, possibly as a pig or, slightly better, a beetle. 'Instead of worshipping one of our modelled idols, if one worshipped the cow one would receive all that is precious in life.' That was Srinivasa's true belief.

Beyond the kitchen area they had their own well with a hand pump and a small enclosed yard where they washed themselves, their clothes and cooking utensils, and where there was a small latrine. The land to the rear stretched some 150 feet. The grey, infertile sandy soil was unsuitable for cultivating vegetables and just a few trees struggled to survive there.

The house itself was of little value, at the most about 2 lakh rupees. The family's greatest asset was the land on which it was built, with its position in the centre of town. However, they would never consider moving. Fifteen people would not only lose a home but also their monthly income from the shopkeepers. Previously most Brahmins in the neighbourhood owned large tracts of land but they had been forced to sell to meet the current escalation in the cost of living. All that still belonged to the Battacharias were 2 acres of land situated some 3 miles away, optimistically called 'rain expecting' land. There was no irrigation or well in the vicinity, and the plot was leased out to tenants who grew paddy and in lieu of rent paid Doraiswamy half the crop. Srinivasa was reluctant even to admit their continued ownership. Two acres was nothing to be proud of.

Although the Battacharias professed an indifference to politics, traditionally most Brahmins vote for the Congress Party regardless of the actual politicians and their ideals. Brahmins rarely discuss whom they supported for fear of losing custom. Uncharacteristically, Srinivasa voted for the more liberal Dravidian (DMK) party. He knew they were being pushed further and further down the economic ladder by measures aimed at eradicating the strength of the caste system, and he believed that this party was the one most likely to halt this process.

In the town there were seven Brahmin families, of which four were custodians of the temple; the heads of the other three households were a teacher, a hotel proprietor and an owner of a tea stall. Each of the priestly families would work in the main temple for a seven-day shift and then have three weeks off, when they would perform weddings and funeral rites, read horoscopes and look after the five other smaller temples in the neighbourhood. Doraiswamy was not on good terms with the family of custodians who lived next door – he still bore a grudge some forty years after Independence ostensibly because they had performed special favours for the District Collector during the days of the Raj. In truth his chilly hostility had more mundane roots. Who not only allowed but encouraged vagrant pigs to stray on to their land? Who blinded their favourite cow ten years ago? The two heads of the families hardly said a word to each other except briefly when handing over the keys of the temple when they changed duty. Doraiswamy's family unit was so tightly knit, and they were all so inflexible in their beliefs, that they found it easier to fraternise, albeit at a distance, with members of the Kshatrya and Banya (Vayshya) castes. This gave them a sense of their own superiority, a confidence in their traditional position in society. Other Brahmins who had similar economic problems were a painful reminder of the realities of life today which they preferred to overlook.

Even though his responsibilities, and the future for his children, were causes for worry, Srinivasa was of a very contented and easy-going disposition.

'What makes for the happiness in my soul are the hopes I have placed in God. I do accept things as they are and tend perhaps to notice my children's smiling faces rather than our adversities. As a priest, too, I come into contact with many kinds of people and I can see that everyone, everywhere, has their worries. We aren't alone. Probably I am the eternal optimist. I believe that our problems will find a way of sorting themselves out.' The only tension he ever felt was that generated by their neighbours.

'Except when my mother and father lose their heads, which I attribute to their advanced years and not being able to comprehend today's problems, there is a generally relaxed and harmonious atmosphere in our family. It has to be like that, otherwise life would be intolerable.' The women, each in their own way, have strong personalities, but it is the men who dominate, their wives' main desire being to look after them and serve them well.

Doraiswamy said the abscess on his scalp was the reason for his shortness of temper. 'I think it's right inside the brain somewhere. Sometimes it gives me the most terrible headaches and it just makes my mood change and sends me off my head. Last year I had an operation and the doctors tried to cut it out.' He went to a nursing home in Chingleput, 15 miles away, where he spent nearly three weeks. He was scared out of his wits so his daughter-in-law stayed with him. It cost them 3,000 rupees, money they had saved up to put towards Jayanti's dowry. On his return home he had to be purified before being allowed to re-enter his own house. He was considered polluted by his contact with the doctors and nurses. Srinivasa chanted a prayer while Krishnaswami sprinkled water on the old man and before his feet as he walked through the entrance porch.

'Actually,' chuckled the old man, 'I know I can lose my head sometimes but it isn't just the operation. Being the eldest everyone depends on me for everything and sometimes it's too much. I can't seem to stop myself from losing my temper even though they all laugh at me. But while I'm alive I am the head of this household and I find the worry of how all my grandchildren are going to manage preys on my mind. For that reason I'm reluctant to let the last bit of land we own be sold. It's all we've got.'

On the days when he was performing temple duty, Srinivasa got up at five o'clock in the morning. He set an alarm clock to wake him so that he could take delivery of the temple milk, used for preparing rice dishes for the gods, which was left on their doorstep – otherwise it could disappear. He then washed, douching himself by the pump using a small brass jar, brushed his teeth and, in his words, 'went for daily needs'. Then he painted special marks on his forehead with thirumanjanam, a sand and clay powder. With great care he drew two white vertical lines, representing the feet of Vishnu, and a red line down the centre, a symbol of Lakshmi, or wealth. Before leaving the house he chanted a mantra, 'Sanjdiyavadanam', getting his thoughts into a suitably devout frame of mind for the tasks ahead of him. This prayer, as well as requesting a purified mental state, also invited the rising sun into the house. Only when this puja had been fully completed and his spirits were in good order would he feel ready to go to the temple. He took no breakfast when he was on duty.

Not only did I sense that it would cause embarrassment if I asked, but it would also have been impractical for me to spend a night with the Battacharia family, so I made arrangements to meet Srinivasa at six o'clock one morning so that I could accompany him to the temple. Large handpainted slogans for local elections adorned the outside wall of this grey stone edifice, along with photographs of the late Mrs Gandhi and the Chief Minister of Tamil Nadu wearing dark glasses. There was a putrid stink near the complex where its walls, set back from the main bus stand, were regularly used as a latrine.

As we entered through the gate, Srinivasa chanted another mantra, directed at the mechanism of the lock and chain on the main door. He then went straight to the main sanctum, swept the floor and cleaned all the idols before going to the temple kitchen to ensure that all the dishes on which they placed the food for the gods were clean. Every day, three intricate and special pujas are performed, and Srinivasa appeared to enjoy the peace of the early morning hours to organise and prepare. It was cool in the large stone courtyard within the temple walls, while inside the two main shrines at the centre of the complex a constant camphor flame made the atmosphere stuffy and suffocating.

Breakfast was prepared and the gods awoken with a dish of rice boiled with milk. All the meals had these same basic ingredients. For the midday dish sugar was added and in the evening some saffron as well. To heighten the belief that these solid edifices were in fact consuming what was offered, Srinivasa hid behind a cloth as he ritually fed the gods. The blackened stone edifice of Vishnu was too large for the main shrine and a hole had had to be carved into one wall so that the idol could be laid down. Now his feet comically stuck through one side. He was lying behind Shiva and was escorted by his two wives, Lakshmi and Bhoomadevi, the goddess of wealth and the goddess of the earth. Before every meal a temple bell was sounded. The familiar hollow ring carried throughout the town and, like the cries from a mosque, enabled the townspeople to identify the time of day. Srinivasa had his own watch, but told me that his father still read the time by the position of the sun.

The first worshippers of the day arrived while the gods were still receiving their breakfast. The remainder of their food was sold to temple devotees for a token price. Its significance was similar to that of the blessed wine and bread taken in communion by Christians as the body and blood of Christ.

When he had fed and cleaned the gods with a paste of tamarind mixed with ash, as there were not many visitors Srinivasa told me he would go home and take a short rest.

'But sometimes the days are hectic, and I may be requested to perform a special puja, an archana, when I will have to chant up to one thousand names of Vishnu. The daily procedure, even during festival time, is always the same. Any members of the public, caste and non-caste Hindus, Muslims, Buddhists and Christians, are allowed to enter the temple if they pay the fifteen paise entry fee.' Later Doraiswamy confessed to me the unease he felt when the Harijans came although he tried not to show his feelings.

Other idols in the temple included Hanuman, the monkey god, Garuda, the vehicle of Vishnu in the form of an eagle, and various reincarnations of Vishnu and Krishna. They were housed in individual shrines, built side by side, similar to a row of prison cells, their metal latticed doors being unlocked three times daily when they were fed. Each god was represented by a sixteenth-century bronze statue, comically clothed in faded white and pink gauze, and at festival time they were all carried to a small parlour to be especially adorned for display. Their jewellery, which belonged to the temple authorities, was stored in a large wooden box. The temple gates were locked at half-past eight every evening, leaving the courtyard empty for the rats to roam and bats to fly. After a day in the temple I was reminded of a visit to Chartres Cathedral in France where I had watched the priest polishing the gold cross and changing the altar cloth, and before each act making a sign of the cross on his forehead and genuflecting before a statue of the Virgin Mary; I noted the similarity of care and attention given to maintaining sanctity.

While Srinivasa worked in the temple, his younger children went to school. In his opinion education was simply a matter of learning to read and write so that one could gain a little independence. Attendance is compulsory in Tamil Nadu if a child lives within the vicinity of a government school.

'I know we're lucky being provided with free education. We just have to pay for their uniforms and text books. They learn their mother tongue, some English, social studies, including some twentieth-century history of India, and maths.'

The teachers came from different castes, and two of them were Harijans. With changing times it was something they had to tolerate and adapt to, but Srinivasa was vexed at the decline in teaching standards. When he was at school the masters were very strict, and he was afraid of them. 'All that has changed. Now they don't prepare their lessons properly and they smoke in the classroom. They no longer seem to care.'

The children came home for lunch at one o'clock, the same time as their father took a break from temple duty, and school resumed for a further two hours in the afternoon. When lessons were finished the boys sometimes played cricket with their friends in front of the temple, or they played marbles or kabardi.

Rajalakshmi, Premamani and Jayanti all worked together in the kitchen. One of them cut the vegetables, another cooked and the third kept the wood fire alight. It was always a joint effort. First they fed Doraiswamy and Kamala, then Srinivasa, Krishnaswami and the children, and when everyone had finished they ate what was left. They cooked only simple meals, without a great variety of dishes, and kept to a very strict form of vegetarianism, the bulk of their diet being rice, boiled vegetables and wheat. They used milk from the buffalo, ghee and a lot of curd (plain yoghurt). Cheese and garlic were not permitted. Breakfast usually consisted of boiled rice with gravy made from boiled squashed black gram mixed with chilli powder, and some vegetables, ghee and curd. Occasionally they made idlis (rice cakes), and puris. The midday and evening meals were similar. For a sweet dish, flesh from the coconut was mixed with vermicelli and sugar, or a puree was made with rice, dal and sugar. Except at festival time, the family spent approximately 100 rupees (about £5) a week on food purchases, to feed fifteen people.

The children were not given hot chilli in their food until they were at least ten years old. They were all breast fed for the first year and then served a bland diet of rice, mixed gram, vegetables and curd. The only time the family ever ate in a restaurant was while making a pilgrimage away from home. Obtaining the correct diet was not a problem as vegetarian eating-houses were always within easy proximity of all the most important temples. None of them had ever eaten in a non-Brahmin household, nor would they accept an invitation to do so, although occasionally Srinivasa would drink tea, coffee or a bottled drink at a neighbour's stall.

Although his father had vague memories of a food shortage during the Second World War, Srinivasa had never experienced hunger. He had always been able to feed his family, foregoing out-of-season fruits and vegetables when resources were low. He could borrow a little here and there from a neighbouring shopkeeper, usually the proprietor of the photo-shop, who deducted the amount from his rent, an amicable arrangement for both parties. He was proud, though, and would not admit to being without funds, simply excusing himself by saying that they were awaiting payment for their services already rendered. The women looked after the cash although their husbands both earned and spent it. They had never used a bank and just kept their loose change locked up in a secret corner. Their annual family income was not high enough to warrant paying tax on it – the lowest taxable income in India is 18,000 rupees per year, and only about 4 per cent of the population pay income tax.

During my visits the women were always present, applying themselves to preparing food and keeping the home clean. They told me they rarely left the house. In small towns and villages, trips to the well provided a source of social communication, but they had their own water, and both Rajalakshmi and Premamani were content to talk between themselves and devote their time to caring for their husbands and children. Their little contact with the world outside was confined to attending religious functions and visiting relatives on very rare occasions.

Srinivasa and Krishnaswami did all the shopping, buying the vegetables and cooking materials and purchasing new clothes for their families, even their wives' saris. Occasionally the men visited the barber's shop, but they felt uncomfortable there and so the barber usually came to their house once a week, working in the front entrance porch. He trimmed the younger boys' hair and shaved the older men around their chins, on the tops of their heads and under their arms. Hair was left to grow long at the nape of the neck where it was kept twisted into a small knot. There was no special significance in this style other than that it identified them as working priests in society. Some Brahmin priests in fact shaved all their hair except a very small strand at the back, known as a kudumi.

The kudumi was also left when the heads of their sons were shaved at three, five and seven years of age. The shorn tresses were offered to Vishnu, and were then sold by the temple, sometimes even remodelled into wigs if they were long enough. At the age of ten the boys celebrated the sacred thread ceremony, which symbolised initiation into maturity. Relatives and friends from the same community were invited to share an elaborate meal and special sweets and after a simple puja a local pandit attached the thread. When the boys married, further strands were added to the thread. Inevitably the cotton became soiled so once a year during the Hindu calendar month of Arvana, prior to Krishna's birthday in August, the thread was replaced.

About twice a month Srinivasa or Krishnaswami bought a couple of lottery tickets for just 1 rupee each, although they had never won a prize. The maximum prize in India was 2 crore rupees (20 million rupees or £1 million), and they were optimistic and kept hoping. 'What a pleasure to win. All our dowries could be accounted for!' They watched their budget with great care. As with many families in rural India, new clothes were purchased about twice a year, usually at festival times. The men wore veshti and jhundu, coloured cotton shawls which they draped gracefully over their shoulders, and a dhoti wrapped around their thighs. These garments were kept immaculately clean and well pressed by the local dhobi. Srinivasa wore a thulasi around his neck, a copy of the necklace worn by the gods in their temple.

'We may spend up to a thousand rupees on new clothes at a time, but that is for fifteen people. We need a lot of saris and dhotis, and we have to buy something for everyone or else there is complaining. We have to spend three hundred rupees every year on school clothes too. We never purchase jewellery. We can't afford such luxury. What little we have is inherited.' The village tailor used to make sari blouses for the women before Jayanti learnt to use an electric sewing machine on which she also made dresses for the little girls. When funds were short they purchased their clothes by instalment. One of the advantages of living in a small community was being able to offer the cloth merchants their priestly services in exchange for a few yards of cotton. Srinivasa would never wear leather shoes but he had relaxed his attitudes towards his children's footwear, acknowledging the need for some protection from broken glass in the square outside and appreciating that sandals made from leather were the most hardwearing. He convinced himself that the hide had been taken from a cow which had died a natural death, and insisted that all footwear should be kept outside their house in the entrance porch.

When the women had their monthly periods they rested quietly in the back yard for three days. During the rainy months this could be quite uncomfortable. Their food was served to them on a special plate, and they were forbidden to enter the kitchen at this time. A menstruating woman could physically touch nobody, even caressing her children was condemned, though a few of these taboos were being relaxed and they were permitted to watch a favourite television programme in the evening so long as they sat at a tolerable distance from the rest of the family. With so many people living together, it was quite impractical for them to keep totally segregated. On the fourth day of menstruation, the women took a long ritual bath and performed a special puja to fully cleanse and purify themselves, and their soiled clothes were collected for washing by the dhobi. Washing their own stained garments would make them unclean again.

Not surprisingly, television, which they watched every day, had dramatically altered the structure of their lives. They liked performances of Tamil songs and Tamil melodramas the best and they said they watched the news, although they seemed to absorb little information from it. No one knew who was the president of the United States when I asked, or even of neighbouring Sri Lanka.

Before they had a television, they would settle down to sleep as soon as they had all finished their evening meal, but the entertainment value of the scheduled programmes now dictated the time at which they decided to retire. Mats were rolled out on the floor for everyone except Kamala for whom, as the honoured and respected grandmother, the wood and string charpoy was reserved. Should a husband and wife wish to make love they had to be very subtle. The husband normally made his wishes known to his wife as she prepared the sleeping arrangements for her children and then they lay awake, waiting until they were quite sure that everyone was asleep. There was never a suggestion of amorous small talk prior to love-making for fear of disturbing someone else. Only for the first two months of marriage were a couple given any privacy, some time together to learn in private how to handle each other. It was a furtive art, enjoying sex in a room amongst thirteen sleeping bodies.

Every action by every grown member of this family was regarded as a ritual of prayer and duty – preparing and eating a meal, washing and clothing oneself, even making love. Every minute was lived in the hope that, as the highest born, this would be their final journey in this world. If their lives were conducted with truth and devotion, they would finally attain the cherished state of nirvana. But current harsh economic realities posed problems for which no solutions were to be found through their religious work. Srinivasa believed it was wrong for a priest to demand too much money for his services. People gave what they knew in their hearts they could afford and he never harassed devotees, never compelled them to pay more. Payment was always left to the will and pleasure of the party concerned, although 2 rupees was the minimum they could realistically accept. On a couple of occasions, much to his delight, Srinivasa was paid 100 rupees.

The Battacharias were paid a fixed salary of 30 rupees a month by the temple authorities from a small government donation intended also to cover the purchase of rice, the food for the gods. A hundred rupees came from rent dues and the rest of their income was made up from a variety of small fees for their other priestly services.

When he accompanied his father on temple duty, Ravi was given money by devotees which he immediately handed over, though sometimes Srinivasa gave him back a few rupees. Then he took his old school friends to see a film in the local cinema. They all liked good Tamil adventures. Being with them reminded him of what he was missing.

'I don't really want to be a priest for the rest of my life,' he confided. 'My friends work at various jobs, helping in shops, driving rickshaws. I'd really like to be an engineer.' I often saw him sitting in the radio shop watching the owner repairing faulty TV sets, and he reckoned he could fix up all kinds of electrical wiring and installations. Many of his contemporaries were married too, but, should he continue his apprenticeship, he would have to wait for another eight years, when he had fully learnt all the necessary priestly duties, before he could contemplate marriage.

'Ravi started to help in the temple kitchen five years ago, when he was fifteen years old. He learns the rituals by watching and assisting me and his grandfather, day by day observing all the functions, picking up the relevant mantras. Although there is no set time for this apprenticeship, no special service of ordination, it usually takes about ten years to learn everything and fully absorb all the duties he will have to perform if he decides to become fully active in this profession. But I am beginning to doubt the likelihood of any of my children being able to follow my profession, even if they want to,' confided Srinivasa. 'There is less and less opportunity for this kind

131

of work. Maybe with the kind of education they are now having they will do some office work, but they could be the first generation of my family not to work in the temple.'

Srinivasa knew how to read horoscopes but refrained from doing so while his father was still alive. Anyone needing this service would always refer to the eldest priest in the household, believing that his experience and wisdom enabled him to give the most accurate reading. Doraiswamy's horoscope reference books were vital to his priestly function and family income, so he kept them out of the reach of his youngest grandchildren on a wooden slab strung up to one of the beams in the living room. 'But I'm losing my sight now. I can't go on reading them much longer. I know my son will be quite reliable when he takes over from me though I doubt Ravi will learn. He'd rather be at the movies.'

These horoscopes are available in any good book store in the large cities of India but superstition decrees that to ensure an accurate and healthy reading one always has to consult and pay a Brahmin. One can reap unfortunate mistakes through self-astrology. It is the duty of all Hindus to maintain the welfare of the priest, the absolute upholder of the faith, and not allow him ever to be reduced to the state of a beggar. He must always, however meagre his circumstances, be held in honour by his devotees and be enabled to keep body and soul together with a fair degree of dignity.

When reading a horoscope for a possible marriage Doraiswamy studied ten signs for the boy and the girl respectively, and, of these ten pairs, seven had to complement each other for the couple to be compatible. It was a case of complicated mathematics using the dates and times of their births. For this service he was usually paid 5 rupees. Sometimes, if he had a good reading, a customer would pay 10 rupees because he was so relieved, but then if he was disappointed he might only offer 2. It was up to the priest to be honest and not misread his script, because after all, his livelihood depended on a reputation of being thorough and fair. I asked him if he had ever used a calculator and he looked up at me with a twinkle in his eye. 'I've been tempted but then I think I would be accused of cheating and I wouldn't get a decent fee.'

Attendance at a marriage ceremony could be a twelve-hour

commitment for the Brahmin priest. The proceedings would start one evening and the actual wedding, a ritual of about two hours, would take place the following morning. Again the horoscope would be consulted to find the most auspicious hour for the Phere, when the couple walk around a holy fire seven times to ensure that all the vows are sanctified, and when promises are made to the gods of eternal betrothal, and protection is requested from all the spirits. These vows would be chanted by the priest in Sanskrit and completed by the groom tying a holy thread around the neck of the bride. The fee for performing a marriage was a minimum of 25 rupees and could be as much as 100 rupees.

When a Brahmin attended a Harijan wedding he would keep a physical distance from the bride, the groom and their families. Out of economic necessity Doraiswamy read their horoscopes and advised them on a suitable day for the marriage to take place but to date Srinivasa had never attended a Harijan wedding. He would not even enter the living quarters of scheduled castes to perform their rituals with them. 'In Tamil Nadu many Harijans have appointed their own priests, Valluvars, from families living within their community,' said Srinivasa, when he saw the look of surprise on my face.

He continued to explain to me the rituals enacted in the other duties. 'When someone dies the priest is always requested to assist in the funeral rites. When a Brahmin dies funeral preparations have to commence immediately as evil spirits are believed to enter the body as the soul departs. The maximum time a dead body can remain in a house is twelve hours. All normal life as such ceases until the funeral procedures have been completed. Although word will be sent out, the immediate family of the dead man won't wait for the arrival of the other relatives. The shrouded body is taken to the sea shore and the ceremonial rites commence. The following day the family returns to the same spot and sprinkles the smouldering ashes with a little milk. When they are cool enough these ashes are collected together, put into a clay pot and kept for a further sixteen days before the family returns to the beach and performs a final farewell, tipping all the remnants into the ocean.

'If my father happens to die before my mother, after the funeral she will return to the house for sixteen days,' explained Srinivasa. 'My wife will fix flowers in her hair and she will wear her best and most colourful saris. At midnight on the last day, neighbouring widows from the same community will come and collect her and lead her to the sea shore. They will cut the holy marriage thread from her neck and shave her hair. From the seventeenth day she will be officially a widow. For the rest of her days her hair will be kept closely cropped, she will no longer paint a red tilaka on her forehead or wear a coloured sari, in some cases not even the blouse, but will just wrap a plain cloth around her body.' As I looked at Doraiswamy's wife crouched on the floor, her eyes closed and head cradled in her bony arms, I thought it unlikely that she would outlive her husband.

Dhamo later told me that in their community a widow is forbidden to remarry, but a widower is permitted to find another wife.

This was a religious neighbourhood so the priests were kept occupied. Sometimes Srinivasa travelled by bus to visit families but he usually walked because the buses did not go to the smaller villages and the three men in the family had to share one bicycle.

'I walk an average of four miles a day. Not much, you may say, but in the hot months it really can use up your energy, especially when you have to concentrate during the puja. It wouldn't do for a priest to fall asleep while performing his duties!' laughed Srinivasa. Then he told me in hushed tones about the subtle ritual of Manjemeratu, when a young girl's first period was celebrated. It was pronouncement that she was ready for marriage. The house in which the girl had just reached her physical maturity was regarded as being at its most polluted and the priest had to bless the home when it had been cleaned.

Some of the wealthier families in the town often asked the priest to say a special puja in their home during festivals. Krishna's birthday, Krishnayanti, celebrated in August, was followed in September by the birthday of Ganesh, Vilayakasadhurthi, and the birthday of Rama (an incarnation of Vishnu) in November, which usually coincided with Diwali, the Hindu New Year. The most popular and colourful of family festivals in South India was the harvest festival of Sankranti which lasted four days in January. At the end of March there was a floating festival, Masimagam, during which a procession of devotees accompanied idols of Sreedevi and Bhoomadevi, incarnations of Vishnu's consort Lakshmi, for a dip in the ocean. The main local temple festival was Brahmomautchvaram celebrated at the end of April and lasting ten days. On the seventh day a statue of Vishnu was placed on the temple chariot and pulled around the town square. There were no festivals during the summer months. The intense heat and the early monsoon in this region were counterproductive to gaiety and celebration.

Rameshwara, a celebration of the lunar eclipse, fell during the period I was visiting the family. As the sun set, Srinivasa and Krishnaswami took their wives and children to the sea shore. When the moon started to rise the two priests took a handful of holy grass and tossed it into the ocean to rid them all of any lurking bad spirit. They all joined hands and carefully immersed themselves in the waves. Then, their dripping clothes clinging to their wet bodies, they walked back home.

'All of us believe, absolutely, in rebirth. There's certainly no doubt at all in my mind although I cannot recall my behaviour and circumstances of a former life. Something, somewhere in my soul, tells me that I conducted myself in such a manner to be rewarded accordingly.' In Srinivasa's opinion bad deeds included smoking, drinking alcohol, eating beef, pork or any other kind of meat. Social misdemeanours such as cheating and stealing were lesser crimes. In their small town there was little serious crime, only the occasional petty pilfering.

'In my daily prayers', he continued, 'I ask for the whole family to be kept well and that my children study well. I never request money or extra material wealth.'

Srinivasa conceded that it was rare now to find three generations of priests in one family. Only the old style Zaminders, wealthy landowners, could afford to keep their families together. Srinivasa wanted his children to get the best education available and to survive it was likely they would eventually be compelled to leave this small town and find work elsewhere. The elder son of the custodian who lived next door was now working in the traffic police in Madras and the younger son was an engineer working in a large national company which manufactured spare parts for lorries and automobiles.

135

On the bus ride to Madras I kept thinking about Doraiswamy's parting words. The last time I saw him he had a bad headache. He lay back in his chair, his feet pulled up on the seat and his right hand stroking his forehead. He found it painful to think about the future and he let out a long sigh as he looked at me.

'I'll tell you something about my grandchildren,' he lamented. 'Once they know how to read and write they will run away.' There was little I could say apart from to offer my thanks for his family's goodwill and cooperation, as I knew he was probably right.

29 Doraiswamy meditates during the day while his wife sleeps beside him
30 Consulting a horoscope   31 Having served the gods their breakfast,
Srinivasa takes a rest at the feet of Vishnu

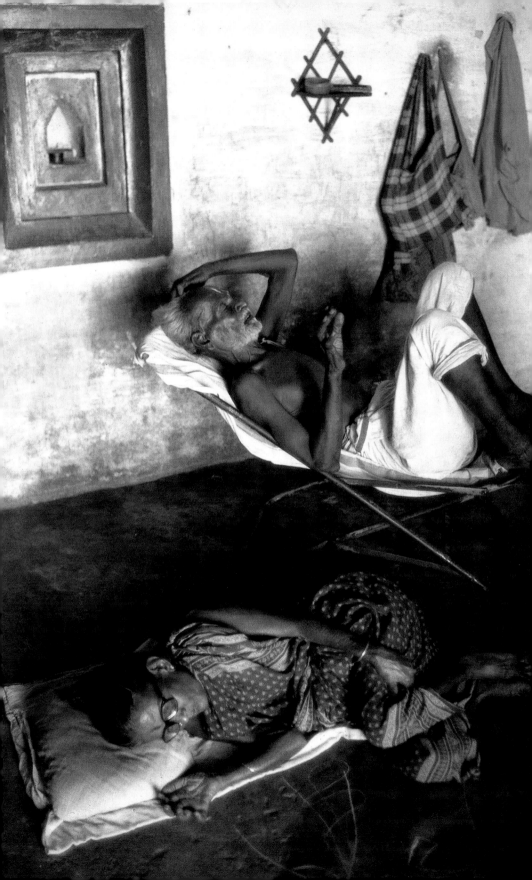

32 The cow is the true living incarnation of all the gods, and its framed portrait can be seen hanging in many households. The gods depicted in this kitsch reproduction are as follows:

In the bridge of the nose – *Sivan (Shiva)*
In the nostrils – *Murugan* and *Ganesh*, two sons of *Shiva*
In the horns – *Veman* and *Indran*, two bodyguards of *Vishnu*
In the ears – *Aswini* and *Kumarar*, gods of sound
In the throat – *Ragu*, a protector from evil, in the form of a tortoise
In the top of the thigh – *Vishnu*
In the hump – *Bhirammah (Brahma)*
In the left front leg – *Maruthi*, or *Hanuman*, the monkey god
In the right front leg – *Bhairavan*, protector of villages, an
    incarnation of *Shiva*
In the four hooves – the *Himachal Bharvatham*, a range of mountains
    where remedial herbs are cultivated
In the body – *Saraswathi*, the goddess of learning and art,
    Bhoomadevi, goddess of the earth, *Agni*, god of fire, *Varunan*, god
    of rain, *Gubern*, the god with great riches endowed with blessings
    from *Lakshmi*, *Bharathuvasar*, the holy saint who composed
    four songs of the Vedas, accompanied by *Vasistar*, *Viswamitrar*
    and *Barasarar*, *Lakshmi* herself, goddess of wealth, *Gangadevi*,
    goddess of the rivers, *Naradar*, mediator in the universe, and the
    Janagakumararcal, disciples of holy saints who composed the
    Vedas
In the udder – *Amirthasagaram*
In the tail – *Nagarajan*, a representative of evil that has to be
    overcome
In the tip of the tail – *Sri Hanar*, the god of cleanliness

7

A Harijan Family
in Bihar

Bihar, a state in northern India, touches heavily on the conscience of the Indian people. The plains to the south of the Himalayas take the brunt of a harsh and cruel climate. They are persistently beset either by years of parching drought or, paradoxically, by raging floods, which with monotonous regularity cause havoc, destroying homes, crops and livestock, and often taking human lives too. Moreover, the area's political system, firmly entrenched in caste and impenetrable corruption, does little to relieve the prevailing poverty and rampant exploitation of farm workers. Those in government at a local level prefer to discourage education and mobility among the rural population in an attempt to maintain their hold over so-called democracy.

In midsummer, despite rumours of an early monsoon in the coastal regions, Bihar is gripped by a stifling heat. Those living in the villages swelter through the early weeks of June, a mental thirst anticipating those first sweet drops of relief as a thick batch of cloud gathers overhead, momentarily cutting out the intense glare of the midsummer sun. The temperatures, however, tenaciously refuse to fall, and even as darkness comes there is little relief. Starless nights clamp the earth in a vice of thick cloying heat. Without electricity there are no overhead fans to cool the air. There is little work to do on the land. Already tilled, sown and partially harvested in the preceding months, acre upon parched acre lies, without efficient means of irrigation, totally infertile. Though often full to overflowing, before the monsoon the tributaries of the nearby River Ganges are reduced to a mere trickle.

Patna, a city of some two million inhabitants and 25,000 cycle-rickshaws, is the capital of Bihar. I had the good fortune to have made friends with a correspondent who was working there for a national newspaper. Prior to his becoming a journalist he had studied sociology and he was eager to help with my project. At his suggestion we went to see a member of parliament who was something of an anachronism in India. He was an opposition member and a Harijan who had managed to overcome the narrow confines of his environment. With fortuitous foresight, his father had ensured that he continued with his studies beyond twelfth grade, and he had won a much-coveted state scholarship to study at university. As a student he had joined a group concerned with the plight of the scheduled castes and from there had entered the political arena, devoting himself to policies which would serve those at the lower end of the social scale. He was an attractive and handsome man whose light brown eyes fixed me with a piercing gaze. I told him I wanted to talk to a Harijan family, and why. He suggested I went to his home town of Hajipur, 20 miles north of the city, where a colleague of his could help us. Then we started to discuss the problems engendered by the caste system and ways in which it could be eradicated. He made a few practical suggestions and then emphatically thumped his hand on his desk.

'The only way to destroy casteism is to make marriage within one's caste unlawful!'

My friend and I looked at one another. Of course this would break down the system but in a democratic society would be impossible to enforce.

To get to Hajipur we had to cross the River Ganges which flowed to the north of the city. The river was about 60 feet deep here and was spanned by the longest bridge in the whole of Asia. Named after the Mahatma Gandhi the bridge rose high over the holy river and its banks to ensure that the construction would withstand the most savage of monsoon rains. Since it first opened, it had carried a continual stream of long-distance heavy goods vehicles, trucks, cars, motor-rickshaws and horse-carts, heading northward to the Nepalese border on the one completed section, protected on only one side by a parapet. The eastern section was still a mass of tangled steel rods and a wide opening revealed a 200-foot drop into the water and paddy fields below. Inevitably there have been fatal accidents. Once, a bus with a full load of passengers tried to overtake a speeding motor-rickshaw. The driver swerved, lost control and the vehicle fell off the bridge into the sandy bank of the river. Forty-two people lost their lives. Despite the risk involved the small levy charged is considered a reasonable price to pay, and the bridge has transformed travel and communication between the south and north of the state. However I held on to the edge of the pillion seat of my friend's scooter with fear and trepidation as we faced the oncoming traffic.

Hajipur is a bustling market town and a busy terminus. Hundreds of vultures were perched on a shallow quagmire below the railway line on the road into town, waiting to pick at the refuse discarded by the small cafés serving the main highway. The politician's friend directed us towards the village of Dighi, within easy walking distance, since a third of the population of 450 families there were Harijans and we would be bound to encounter a suitable family for my research. We approached the village along an avenue of tamarind and guava trees through acres of banana groves. Sixty-foot-high toddy palms stood noble and upright on the borders of the surrounding paddy fields below the main railway line running from the ancient Mughal capital of Lucknow eastwards to the hills of Assam. I found it a gentle, soft location, a camouflage for the constant grinding poverty which I was about to discover prevailed among its inhabitants.

Under the shade of a large banyan tree, a group of farmers were gathered around a man seated at a small table, on which was spread a well-thumbed and frayed ordinance survey map. The local surveyor had been summoned to sort out a dispute concerning the use of a ditch. My friend and I waited for the meeting to conclude.

I noticed a small boy emerging backwards on all fours from the doorway of a nearby house, carefully manoeuvring himself over the wooden threshold. He ran his fingers up the plastered walls and pulled himself upright. As he stood, he turned round and lifted his face to the light. I thought he smiled when he saw me. I went to where he was standing and then saw that his eyes were enlarged and swollen and the pupils were filled with a smoky blue opaque film. He couldn't see me at all but had probably heard someone remark on my arrival. Behind him a woman was crouching, another child squatting between her legs, while her fingers deftly felt through his thick black hair, squeezing out the eggs of headlice. She noticed my staring at her sightless son and beckoned me over to sit beside her. With my friend acting as an interpreter, she quickly filled me in on the history of her little boy's plight and later I ascertained she had thought I had come to cure her son.

'It happened about a year ago during the colder weather. Kishan's eyes started to water. They itched and hurt him a lot, so he just kept them shut. We didn't take much notice because all the children in the village had heavy head-colds that winter. Yet he didn't cough and his nose wasn't blocked; just his eyes wouldn't stop watering. When he told me that some sand or grit had got into them, I made a paste of grass and water and gently rubbed it on to the affected areas. He found that quite soothing but they didn't get any better. After a month we walked to the nearest medicine shop in Hajipur, to purchase a small tin of ointment. The remedy, however, produced no improvement. In fact Kishan's eyes felt only worse, and he would sit all day keeping them closed, covering them with his hands quietly moaning and beating his head against a wall.

'Then he said that when he did open his eyes everything in front of them was getting blurred and hazy. We were bewildered and confused as to what we should do next. We took advice from a neighbour. There was a large hospital at Muzzafarpur, over forty miles away, where there were doctors who could perform miracles and cure all kinds of ailments. My husband had just enough money for the bus for himself, the boy and me and a little to spare, twenty rupees, enough to pay for treatment, we thought.

'It was the first time I had travelled out of the neighbourhood, let alone visited a large town, but I was too anxious about my son's health to take in the surroundings. On arrival at the bus terminus we asked the way to the hospital and instead were directed down a small alley to a private eye clinic. A man in a white coat who

141

appeared to be in charge inspected Kishan but didn't tell me what was wrong. He gave me another tube of ointment and took our twenty rupees, giving us the impression he was doing us a favour. Back home I rubbed in some ointment every day, and within a week he said the pain had gone, but now he couldn't see anything at all.'

The bewildered woman stopped talking as she saw her husband come towards us. The meeting was over. The surveyor had sorted out the dispute, got on his bicycle and left. The husband introduced himself to me. He was an agricultural labourer, Ramashray, and his wife was Manojma. Before explaining the reason for my visit to their village I persuaded Manojma to finish her story.

Growing desperate, she continued, she had persuaded Ramashray to take Kishan to the hospital again. This time he found the right building and was seen by a trained specialist who could detect no response when he shone his torch on to the opaque pupils. He came straight to the point. Kishan's eyes had been destroyed by conjunctivitis. Tragically, if he had been treated correctly at the outset the infection would have cleared up immediately, but because the child had rubbed his itching eyes an infection had set in and now the sight was probably beyond restoring. The specialist gave the boy an injection and some more ointment to stop any further infection. He also made a vague reference to a course of treatment or an operation that the child could have when he was more physically developed. Then he asked for 200 rupees.

Ramashray panicked. Such a huge sum was nearly a quarter of what he earned in six months. The doctor gave him a chit stating that before a course of treatment could be undertaken at that hospital the fee should be paid, and Kishan's mother doubted that they would ever be able to afford it.

'It's difficult trying to remember the sequence of events. Everyone we spoke to said something different. We haven't any money so we just do our best and see anyone who is available. There's a government eye doctor who comes to the village about every six months, and he has said that there's nothing he can do for Kishan. Besides, he told me that it is not his kind of problem. I told him that I could see the eye contracting when I shone a light in it, and he said that maybe my son could have an operation. I've seen something move right inside his eye, so deep down inside I know he'll be all right. Now that the itching has stopped it's just a matter of weeks before he'll see again. Every day I wait for it to get dark so that I can start my experiment of flashing a kerosene lamp in front of his face.' She paused and stared at me. I saw tears welling up in her eyes. I nodded at her in sympathy and with difficulty quietly explained that I had no medical qualifications but that when I returned to Patna I would talk to a doctor. When I told them the nature of my visit I asked if they knew of a suitable family living in their neighbourhood. Ramashray thought for a while, then bobbed his head from side to side. He pulled himself up with pride and told me his late father had once occupied the honoured position of being the Sardar, the headman, of his community. He was the youngest of his five sons so surely there could be no better family to talk to than his.

And so we sat down together and I jotted down family particulars in my notebook. As I wrote, their other children gathered around my feet looking up at me with trusting faces, watching every move I made. They studied me intently and I suddenly felt embarrassed by the expensive-looking Swiss gold watch I was wearing. Kishan enjoyed working the mechanism on my tape recorder and was fascinated to hear his own voice played back to him. When the daylight began to fade we made arrangements for my return.

An English colleague who read the first draft of this chapter told me he thought I was very tough on peasant rural India. He recognised everything I saw but our spectacles had different coloured lenses. While he took in his stride the grime, the filth and the poverty, I obviously hated it. In my descriptions he didn't get the sense of survivors but of a people dying and of my sorrow for them. Inevitably my observations came from my own cultural point of view and at times I felt emotionally drained by my efforts to accept the plight of these fine but suppressed individuals, but I trust this will not read as a portrait in pity. On the contrary, I found this first encounter and my following visits to Dighi provided me with the most moving and profoundly affecting moments of all my visits to India while writing this book. I greatly admired the uncomplaining dignity of Ramashray and his family and I was deeply touched by their openness and the warmth they gave me.

It was nearly eighteen years since Ramashray and Manojma first met. Manojma's father, an employee of the Indian Railways, came to the village of Dighi to look for a husband for his daughter. As Ramashray had more education than most of his contemporaries in his community he seemed a suitable candidate. The young man was delighted to be offered a bicycle as a dowry, seeing it as a status symbol. He dreamed of getting married, and of proudly cycling to college to continue his studies. He did not meet his bride before the marriage took place, in fact he wasn't even shown a photograph of her, yet brimming over with enthusiasm he took all his brothers, their wives and his cousins, a large party of more than sixty people, to attend his wedding in Manojma's village, 5 miles away. After a simple Hindu ceremony, his surprised in-laws had to feed them all.

'I didn't feel anything when I first met Ramashray, and I certainly didn't think there was anything special about it,' said his wife, having taken their introduction in a quite matter-of-fact way. For her, marriage was just one of those things that happened; one didn't question one's father's choice. Unfortunately as soon as Ramashray was married his father found that he was unable to support the couple, and so Ramashray had to abandon his dreams and leave college to look for work in order to feed himself and his new wife. Months later, the cycle was sold to pay off an outstanding debt.

Ramashray worked when he could as an agricultural labourer. He was in his late thirties when I met the family and his wife was about five years his junior.

Before her marriage her name was Mudri Devi. It was their custom to name a new wife by adding a prefix to her husband's name, and then when she started her family to call her the mother of the first child, and so she was now affectionately referred to as Manojma. She remembered how before their first child arrived they were both so shy with each other that they avoided talk between themselves if anyone else was around.

'I got married quite late. The education of my four brothers was more important than my dowry and my parents waited until I was eighteen or nineteen. My father spent all his spare money on the boys. Two of them have managed to better themselves. One is a mechanic and one teaches in a village somewhere, a place similar to here, but being the only girl I was taught nothing. I am unable to read let alone write my own name. I don't know how long I've been married. For fifteen, twenty years?' she puzzled.

Baffled by the simplest addition and subtraction, Manojma could not work out how old she might be. The lines etched on her forehead and around her mouth were evidence of the many strains she had endured. Yet she was still bright-eyed, her face eager as she talked. She crouched on her haunches like a wild bird, spreading her sari over her thin arms and around her children, holding the smallest between her knees as she caressed them all, gently stroking their faces with her tiny, bony hands. Their father, too, was affectionate and tactile with them all, especially little Kishan.

Ramashray's eighty-year-old mother, known as Diti (an affectionate term for the work she still did in their community as a midwife) lived with her youngest son. Of the six sons she bore, the five that had survived all lived in this village.

'I am proud of all my sons. They're all good men, good workers when they get the chance, even though we're often hungry,' she told me. She was a tiny, sparrow-like woman, shrivelled in her old age. Her arms and legs were covered in tattoos. I asked her what they represented but the patterns had shrunk along with her own body and she had forgotten.

'I know I look frail but I'm very strong, and I'm still asked to help with deliveries when there are complications' – she grabbed hold of my arm and squeezed it to show her strength. Most of the time I was with the family she spent sleeping on a charpoy at the back of the house. She had lived well beyond the average life expectancy and was thought to be the oldest living member of their community; her sons were puzzled as to why it was she was still alive.

'She's old, tired and hungry, and the small monthly pension of thirty rupees she gets from the government certainly isn't enough to look after her. She's really ready to die and we're waiting for her to go too. It somehow isn't right to live for such a long time when one is just a burden on one's family,' Ramashray complained, 'but I suppose it has to be God's will that she's kept going, or his way of testing us. Sometimes she wakes up in the morning with a look of surprise on her face at finding herself still alive!'

145

Manojma had given birth to seven children, of whom four were still alive. Their eldest son, eleven-year-old Manoj Kumar, was a lively boy with a quick, impish smile. They had encouraged him to attend the government classes which were sometimes held in the vicinity, but the boy continually played truant with his friends and wouldn't be tamed despite the fact that he wasn't very fit – he suffered from an enlarged thyroid gland in his neck, the result of an iodine deficiency caused by malnutrition. By contrast, his seven-year-old sister Tetri had a timid and serious nature. In my presence, she often hid in the grimy folds of her mother's sari. Little Kishan also had a twin brother, Binod. The children often squabbled among themselves but their mother told me that this was provoked by a lack of food and, in fact, they loved each other very much. Manojma said she felt especially close to her eldest son.

'I suppose that's normal, him being the first born. Should anything happen to me and my husband, he will be responsible for his sister and younger brothers. I really want him to study hard now so that he can get a steady job when he grows up and not have to rely on the whim of a landlord like his father has to.'

Manojma lost three sons. Two died of dysentery when they were small babies and the second son, Sonu, died when he was seven years old from a parasite infection, kala-azar, contracted from drinking infected water. Although it is curable, the disease was rampant in this locality. If the sufferer goes without treatment, the spleen enlarges causing high fever and anaemia, hence malnutrition and death.

Ramashray remembered he had a good job at the time, selling bananas. 'I became so nervous, and frightened that all the other children would die too that I got confused with the money I was supposed to collect and was fired. I have thought about practising some kind of family planning but if I have a vasectomy I will lose my strength. I'm a small man with many mouths to feed: if I lose my vigour, how will I be able to work hard so that I can buy food? Anyway, Manojma isn't interested. She thinks that God works out these things for you, in the same way that he has taken away three of our sons.'

Manojma did once ask a doctor if she should be sterilised but he told her she was too weak and anaemic to have the operation. She was convinced that anaemia meant she had too little blood in her body.

'I so hated it when we lost Sonu. I felt completely bewildered and lost. Sometimes, when I was alone in the house, I would find tears welling up inside me. I still panic even thinking about it. I have this terrible fear that it could happen again to one of the others.

'I fed all the children myself for about two years. In fact they hardly ate any solid food until they came off the breast. Someone told me that that was why they were undernourished, but then someone else would say that mother's milk is the best, so who is one to believe? Anyway, feeding them myself seemed to act as some kind of birth control and meant one mouth less to purchase rice for. My problem is that when I feed a child it drains most of my strength, and I'm still confused as to why I've had so many children who have just died. If they weren't supposed to live, why were they born in the first place, just to make me weak?'

Wood is expensive and a precious commodity and a young death didn't warrant the cost of a coffin, so they buried the two babies close to the railway line near their home. Manojma couldn't remember them very well. At the time she thought she was being punished by God who just made her carry them and give birth and then took them away. When Sonu died, however, they took a boat out on to the holy waters of Konaraghat before burying his remains on the banks of the Gandak, a tributary of the Ganges some 3 miles away.

During her confinements all the family left Manojma alone in the house. Two women, untrained midwives, came from the village, laid some straw on the floor, and then sat with her, silently waiting, sometimes stroking her arms when the pain got bad. If the labour seemed too long, one midwife put her hand up inside Manojma to encourage the head of the child to come out. Sometimes the head of the child tore her as it came out and this would later become infected. She usually gave birth in a squatting position, leaning against one wall, and the baby fell gently on to the straw. When it was a boy everybody was happy, but they were less enthusiastic when it turned out to be a girl. Manojma knew she had been lucky in this respect. She knew some women who, already having daughters, had just wanted to kill their baby girls.

Like Ramashray, most of the men living in their community were agricultural labourers, and there were a few families of Chamars (leather workers) who survived on a small wage paid by the government for sweeping the streets. Their income was supplemented by the traditional task of beating the drum at festivals, weddings and funerals, and by various kinds of leather work such as cobbling and stripping dead carcasses.

The local records showed that Dighi was supplied with electricity but, as in other rural communities, local officials had managed to deflect government funds. A few poles had been placed to carry the supply line but as yet no cables had been laid. Ramashray and his friends said that if they voted it would be for the socialists, the Lok Dal, because that was the party which would ensure the electricity supply was connected.

'I have absolutely no regard for politicians. They just arrive here at election time full of empty promises. I've always supported Indira Gandhi. After all it was she who abolished Untouchability,' he said, confusing her with the Mahatma. He complained that voting was never possible because 'higher caste people' impersonated the villagers and used their voting papers. In India, when a person has voted, his fingernail is marked to prevent him making two votes. When Ramashray and his friends went to the polling station they were told they had already voted. If they showed the men in charge of the booths their clean fingernails they were accused of having removed the ink.

The only medical care was provided by a small government health group which visited the village about once a month. The villagers regarded them with caution and suspicion, a group of opportunists making money out of expensive drugs.

There was no official, regular schooling available. Recently a voluntary teacher had come to the village for a couple of hours each afternoon, and Manojma had attended a few classes. Tetri had started to learn a few letters of the Hindi alphabet. Ramashray said he studied a lot when he was a boy. When his father could afford it, he had persuaded all his sons to attend school. Ramashray had learnt a few words of English, some maths and everyday science, but he had never learnt to read properly and was now only able to write his own name and address. He protested that the need to earn his living and the difficulties of travelling to lessons put a stop to his studies.

'Whatever education I have had doesn't seem to make much difference. I'm just as badly off as my friends who can't do these things. Still, I'll encourage Manoj to learn. With luck things could be different for him. It's not easy, though, because the teacher's visits are so erratic. I've persuaded him to go to some adult education programmes, literacy for the elderly. He is studying with men older than me!' However, the most the boy could do was to write his own name and a few Hindi letters. He couldn't write numbers or even his father's name although he professed he wanted to be a teacher when he grew up.

There were no public latrines in Dighi. To relieve themselves people simply used the open spaces on the outskirts of the village. Three wells each supplied about twenty-five families – in our society that would be the equivalent of more than a hundred people sharing one cold water tap for all their household use. Nobody could recall any of the wells running dry although there was often a long wait for the water to collect.

It was a harmonious neighbourhood and the labourers were on friendly terms with the Chamar workers. At festival times they always celebrated and performed their pujas together and shared their food. They helped each other out, lending money when they could, and giving food when anyone had any to spare, which was not often the case. When someone gave, he himself would usually have to go without. Ramashray said he was too proud to ask for help unless he needed money when one of his children was sick. There was always willing cooperation if a man needed a hand rebuilding his house or retiling his roof.

The only crimes in the village were minor thefts. With so many bananas growing around the village, sometimes the temptation was too much and the children grabbed a bunch or two, usually just to fill their empty bellies. If the owners caught them, they were given a sound beating. On occasions a belligerent landowner handed the culprits over to the police and pressed for a conviction. Once, a twelve-year-old boy was sentenced, as a warning to the others, and imprisoned for three years for stealing a couple of bananas.

Often the community would hand out its own justice. If a man was found to be unfaithful to his wife, he was likely to be publicly beaten and then forced to ride on a donkey's back while being jeered. His head would be shaved around the temples, and until it regrew everyone would know what he had done. If he committed the same sin again he could be forced to leave the village and his family for good, despite the economic hardship that would inevitably impose on them. For the same offence a woman received no second chance: she was immediately banned from the village, although within the home it was quite normal for her to joke and chatter in an intimate and sexually teasing manner with her husband's brothers. Generally this relationship was not consummated, but such behaviour sometimes led to physical and sexual contact, which was usually overlooked. Economic dependence on each other encouraged fidelity in this society.

Ramashray's home was well positioned, a few yards from the well. Community meetings were normally held under the banyan tree so he was aware of most activities in the village. He shared his sturdy house with his eldest brother, Jangali, and his sister-in-law and their two sons, although each family lived in two small rooms and fended for itself. The brothers built the house with their father about twenty-five years ago. It was constructed of kutcha, a mixture of mud and plaster, with bamboo rafters and a tiled roof. Ramashray believed that his family had lived on this same site for at least four generations.

Manojma cooked and all the family ate and slept in the front room, where a small clay stove was built into one corner. There were no windows; the only light came through the front door. In this room they kept three metal cooking pots, two metal ladles, four eating dishes and five empty earthenware pots. There were a couple of straw mats, two rag rugs, and Ramashray's tilling tools hung from the eaves. In the back room there were three water buckets and a rush fan. They had one small brass drinking vessel which was a wedding present, four wooden blocks for sitting on, and half a dozen small kerosene bottles which were bought in the village once a month. They hung their few items of clothing on a piece of wire strung from the ceiling. There was no tin trunk for personal possessions because they had none. The only photographs Ramashray had ever owned of himself were taken when he applied for a job in Patna. The family possessed no books, and there were no other records such as birth or marriage certificates. Ramashray boasted that he didn't need a watch for he could tell the time by the position of the sun.

The roof sloped so low that a grown man could only stand upright in the very centre of the house. A glance at the bamboo rafters supporting the roof gave an indication of the damage caused to Manojma's lungs, which manifested itself in a persistent dry cough. The poles were quite black with a residue from the woodsmoke, because of the inadequate ventilation from the entrance door. In construction, priority was given to keeping out the cold during the winter nights and providing respite from the midday sun through the hottest months. During the winter the mud floor got very cold underfoot and at night Manojma laid a few sacks under a straw mat and they all slept together, curling up to each other as close as possible to give each other extra warmth.

Behind the house there was a dilapidated store room constructed of wood and grass with a wooden table on which Diti sometimes slept during the day. Wedged between the table and the walls was her husband's old bicycle, missing most of its vital parts, including the wheels.

Ramashray's simple wardrobe consisted of two checked dhotis, one lunghi, two kurta tops and two vests. He had a pair of leather shoes, which were a gift from a friend who inherited them from his deceased father. Manojma and the children went without shoes, but this didn't bother them. During the summer the smaller children went naked, but at other times they wore shorts which were usually torn and full of holes. At best, Manojma would have two cotton saris. When they started to wear out she would wrap them around Tetri to give her extra warmth.

'Ramashray buys the cloth and I stitch my own blouses and petticoats. I don't know when that last was. Usually I'm stitching and restitching the same blouse all the time, just holding it together. He tries to purchase more clothes as the previous ones wear out, but a new vest or shirt is a luxury for the cold months and will be worn constantly, even at night-time when the temperature falls below ten degrees celsius. Before the winter's end the garment will be torn and full of holes,' she explained.

Manojma owned no jewellery apart from a few plastic bangles and she wore no make-up except occasionally a tilaka on her forehead if Ramashray had managed to purchase a packet of small vermilion felt pads, 1 rupee for twenty-four. She discouraged him from spending money on her. If there was anything to spare she would rather he purchased something for the children.

'Last summer I pawned the only piece of gold my wife still had, a nosepiece. Although it was worth at least two hundred rupees, I got fifty, and I'm being charged interest, but I needed the money too badly to argue.'

Before each of my visits to the family I would go to the local market to buy them small gifts – combs, soap, sweets and coloured pens and paper for the children. Sometimes I would buy Manojma a cotton sari but I was surprised how quickly it would wear out. They accepted these presents graciously but I never had the impression that they expected anything, except for the old grandmother who persistently asked me to bring more biscuits.

When I asked Ramashray for his views on caste and Hinduism he seemed understandably to confuse the two. On the one hand he believed that the caste system was a man-made evil and yet on the other he believed that his present position in society was intended as a penance for some misdeed in a former life. He didn't know what he could have done wrong but it must have been something dreadful to have been reborn into his pitiful condition. His hopes were now for his next life. The only reason he would like to be reborn as a caste Hindu would be to be better off, to own some land and to be able to feed his family. 'I want good food and fine clothes for my wife and children. Kishan lost his sight because I'm a Harijan and have no money, but in my next life none of my children will be blind.' Manojma believed in rebirth too. 'It depends on God what will happen in the next life. I don't think I've done anything bad. I just hope he doesn't put me in the same situation again. The only things I ever dream about are another life with better clothing and better food. I know that rich people and those living in the city are happy having so much, so I'd like to be like them.'

Ramashray said they were never allowed to forget that they were Harijans. 'One feels one's Untouchability most of the time. I've never shared a meal with caste Hindus and I would never draw water from their well. Some of our children do study with theirs but they rarely play together after school. My father used to warn me not to let my shadow fall on a Brahmin. I think perhaps in my subconscious I'm careful in the presence of the high castes, certainly not out of respect but perhaps instinctively. We feel both used and abused by them. I would always avoid any confrontation because then I wouldn't get the work I need to sustain my family. I certainly wouldn't go into the house of one unless invited and I've noticed how sometimes they spray water in my path before I enter. It's insulting, but something one gets used to.

'There is definitely a division between our community and the rest of the village. Fortunately I've never been at the receiving end, although I have seen my neighbours suffering. Recently a barber fell in love with a Kshatrya girl. He was killed by her brothers, but his family were too frightened to inform the police.'

More atrocities were committed in the name of caste in this state than in any other in the whole of India, perhaps an indication that racial tension and police harassment erupted more often in an atmosphere of basic deprivation.

'I think caste violence is a terrible thing,' he continued. 'Some people here have radios, and they tell us about it, but it baffles me. Why should our communities always be the ones to suffer? We Harijans are good people. We care for our families and each other. It's the bullying landlords who create the tensions. I don't really understand them. Maybe they are afraid when Harijans unite. They're just cowards and bullies.'

As an agricultural labourer, Ramashray was seldom paid more than 10 rupees for an eight-hour day (less than 50 pence), the statutory minimum suggested by the government. Unfortunately there was both a shortage of work and an abundance of available and willing hands.

'In the fields I dig, sow, reap and harvest. I'm not very good at ploughing though. I think it's because at five feet four inches I'm too small and can't handle the bullocks. Their necks are so strong

I tend to lose my balance and find it difficult to make the animal go where I want.'

Ramashray worked on average for 160 days in the year, which meant he had to support his family on less than £100 annual income. They managed, but often they didn't eat. Occasionally there was work too for Manojma and even Tetri, sowing paddy. Mother and daughter could work for up to eight hours in the day, bent double, their legs immersed halfway up their calves in parasite-infested soft mud, and between them they would take home 5 rupees. Apart from Tetri, the children rarely worked – there wasn't enough for the grown men, let alone the boys.

A typical day's purchases might include the following: 6 rupees for 2 kilos of rice; 1 rupee for a kilo of potatoes; 2·5 rupees for a litre of kerosene which would last one week, leaving change of half a rupee. One rupee's worth of spices lasted about a week. The government had enforced some control over local food prices although there was outrage at recent price rises without a suggestion in a rise for the minimum wage.

Their basic diet was very simple: roti (leavened bread), satu (minced yellow gram), rice and sometimes a few pickles. During the mango season Ramashray would purchase a few kilos of the unripe fruit from the caretaker of a mango grove just outside the village, cut it up in slices, cover it with salt and chilli and let it dry out on his roof. When it had dried he would add a little vegetable oil and store it inside a large earthen jar. Sometimes he was given a bag of mangoes for working overtime and he could sell off what he didn't need for himself. Once a month, and on special occasions if they could afford it, they might have meat – chicken, goat or lamb. They drank tea only during the cold weather. For the rest of the year they just drank water from the well, but occasionally Ramashray would take toddy, and sometimes he smoked small handrolled bidis. To his knowledge Manojma had never smoked or drunk alcohol. Despite their simple means they were extremely hospitable, embarrassed that they were unable to offer me a plate of food or some warm tea.

Ramashray said he did not have any particular mechanical skills, although he was good with his hands.

'I helped my father build this house, and I can repair the roof. As well as sowing and reaping I know which are the best fertilisers. Science has changed everything since I was a small boy. Now there are several harvests in one year, but I know from experience that the expensive chemical fertilisers they produce in the factories are no better than the ones we prepare ourselves. The best fertiliser is the one we make with dung. We collect it from the cows and buffaloes in the village, store it in a pit, covering it with herbs and grasses, and leave it to ferment. Sometimes we leave it for a year, then it's good and ready to spread over the fields. It is more efficient, cheaper and more easily obtainable than what you can buy. The landlords seem to believe that something that comes in a sack with writing on it is superior, and it's sickening watching them spend money on a load of manufactured rubbish when they don't give us a decent daily wage.'

Ramashray believed that landlords were happy people. 'They are so prosperous and have good houses with all facilities. There's one man I've worked for who lives in the Dharwar area and he owns six hundred acres. Whenever I work for him he only pays us the minimum wage. We never get overtime, despite the government ruling on this. Nobody sticks to it, because they know that if we want more there will always be some worker who will accept less.

'Some landlords can make the most outrageous demands. On days when I am working I have known them to insist that my wife goes to the landlord's house and cleans the floors, and even massages his body, arms and legs, cooks his food and feeds his animals – all without paying her. It's as if he is doing me a favour by giving me work, and thus my family should be grateful and look after him. They'll say, "There's work for you if you can send your wife to my home," and there are men who employ us regularly who expect us to help them when there's a special occasion in their family, a wedding or a birth to celebrate. They don't pay us either, but if we're lucky we are given some of the food that isn't eaten. It's such a difficult thing, you know, when you've got four hungry children, to be defiant towards a landlord when he takes advantage. How can you? – the way they look at you sometimes with their pleading eyes, and I know their stomachs are empty. But then sometimes there are cakes and sweetmeats I can bring home for them.'

155

Ramashray and his friends seemed interested in the idea of a movement for better pay and conditions but they couldn't see it happening. The might of the landlord was too strong.

In the community everyone was as well off or, rather, as badly off as each other. Nobody shirked or was lazy, since nobody wished to go without food.

'I can't afford to be ill, ever. If I can't work my family won't eat. I've got a liver complaint at the moment,' he said, pulling at the skin below one eye to show his yellow jaundiced eyeball. 'I know I should eat some radishes or sugar-cane but I just can't afford them.

'I'm not lazy. It may seem that we are considering the amount of time we spend sitting around, but that's not out of choice. In truth a Harijan can't afford to be lazy, but we take life at a slower pace when it's very hot. If there is work to be done we simply start earlier in the morning, having a long break during the hottest hours, and then work into the evening. Towards the end of the dry season we all work very hard preparing our homes for the rain, making sure that the roof is solid and waterproof.

'When I work I get really hungry. Of course I get hungry too when I'm not working, but I can't think about food then because there isn't any money. If I go to work without having eaten sufficient food I begin to feel very weak. But because I need the work I always pray that my employer won't notice and compare my effort to that of others.'

Ramashray told me he was a practising Hindu. 'I think about God whenever there is a crisis and silently I say a little prayer to myself, usually asking for some work. Always I ask for someone to give us a better tomorrow. Often my prayers are a form of protest. Why can't he give me more work? After all, I'm an able man. Actually I blame him for everything that is wrong in my life, and as you can see that's just about everything. Goodness, I have cursed him sometimes!'

Manojma didn't pray regularly, just at festival time, when she made a brief puja at their make-shift shrine at home for her children to have good health.

Like many Christians in the West today, the family used religion as a prop, a pillar to lean on, for example when a close relative died. On such an occasion, there was fasting for twenty-four hours before some rice and milk were boiled together and tasted. As a mark of respect, and to show the strength of attachment to the deceased, most of the meal was thrown away, a sacrifice indeed for those who regularly did not have enough to fill their bellies. On the third day the sons of the deceased separated themselves from their families for a further thirteen days, and at the end of this period a Brahmin priest was invited to the house to perform an act of purification so that the men could again have physical contact with their wives and children. The priest would accept payment only in the form of rupees or articles of clothing. The final gesture to the departed was to prepare rice balls, spiritual food to sustain the deceased's soul on its journey to heaven.

When Ramashray's father died his family had prepared a large feast after the funeral because of the important position he had held in the community, and they had to pay the priest 200 rupees. 'Imagine being able to earn that kind of money for half a day's work, most of which was spent eating our food! He made us feel that if we didn't pay him all the money, my father's soul would suffer in some way. Maybe it would hinder his chances in his next life. There was no money with which to pay him outright, so we had to promise that we would settle the debt as soon as we could. Maybe I've been born a Harijan because my children in my former life didn't give me a proper funeral?' Shortly after his father's death Ramashray enjoyed a brief stint working in Calcutta, to some a city of living hell but to a Bihari peasant a Mecca of opportunity and wealth. He returned home because he felt lonely.

Yet, despite the unrelenting worry of finding work, what Ramashray could take for granted was the stability of living within an open and friendly community, where there was always a sympathetic and understanding neighbour with whom he could commiserate when the going got rough. He was not the only man who fretted at night worrying about feeding his family, Manojma was not the only woman to have lost her children, Kishan was not even the only child in the village to have lost his sight. They were not alienated by their problems. Even Ramashray admitted that there were times of the year when his spirits lifted, when a better life seemed a possibility.

'I am a simple person. A good day's work, a full stomach, plenty to eat for Manojma and the children – then I am a happy man.'

The constant lack of food, little outside stimulation and few possibilities for receiving basic skills in reading and writing prevented the younger generation questioning their condition. The children had never had any toys apart from a few marbles. They played a form of hopscotch with sticks and stones. Before my visit they had never had the opportunity to paint or draw, for their parents could not afford to purchase paper and pens. Manoj boasted that he could swim, but he confused it with playing in the water, bathing in small reservoirs created by heavy monsoon rains. He had never seen television and had seen a radio only once, and had shown no curiosity to listen to it.

The two main festivals celebrated in the village were Kartignum in October, for the worship of the sun, and Holi, the spring festival. Spring was Manojma's favourite time of the year. The nights were warm but the days were still not too hot and there was regular work for Ramashray.

'Sometimes we make a pilgrimage to the banks of the Ganges and give small offerings to the rising and setting sun. If we can afford it at the time we may buy some meat, clothes for the children, a dhoti for me and a new sari for Manojma – but perhaps all four is wishful thinking. During Diwali, the Hindu New Year, we light as many candles as we can afford to purchase and decorate our home with leaves from mango tree.'

The start of the rainy season was a joyous time for everyone in the village – a time when the blessed rains fell in abundance, filling the rice fields. I saw buffaloes immersed in wet, muddy trenches wallowing with delight, long-necked white egrets cheekily perched on their half-submerged buttocks. An abundance of bright green shoots of paddy and young wheat replaced the dry scorched soil of the summer months. The villagers at first delighted in this bounty from the skies, but as the weeks passed, and thick dark grey clouds rolled overhead, farmers nervously watched for a break in the ceaseless downpour as they saw their lands slowly become water-logged quagmires of mud, awash with spoiled crops. Every householder prayed then that the river wouldn't burst its bank and threaten the foundations of their homes.

Towards the end of the rainy season the entire community celebrated a special puja for Shavani, an incarnation of the goddess Durga, and they invited me to join them in their feasting. As dawn broke a special meal was prepared, a curious dish of chopped banana, onion and black gram, served on a bright green banana leaf. A white billy-goat, soon to be ceremoniously decapitated, was given a taste before the mixture was handed out to all the children. The hapless animal, whose flesh was to be eaten that same evening, was then held tightly by the thighs under an arbour of bamboo and ashok leaves and with one quick stroke its head was removed, the body left quivering for a full five minutes, almost threatening to get up headless and run away. This was a prelude to a day full of worship and rejoicing. The womenfolk donned their gayest saris, ceremonial fires were lit, offerings were made in their small temple, a group of musicians rhythmically banged the drum and clashed the cymbals, and everyone clapped their hands and sang: 'Life is just like a river – swift current, strong flow and God on the other side. We will cross this river to meet Him, our ultimate goal.' As the oldest woman in the community, Diti anointed bamboo poles with a rice and milk paste and to these poles were attached flags depicting the goddess of strength. Every household had contributed 12 rupees to the day's celebrations. In the morning Ramashray had had his bi-monthly shave. The barber had wanted 50 paise for his services, but Ramashray had given him 30. 'You didn't use any soap!' he had scolded.

When I spent a night in the village in early March I was treated with great respect and one of Ramashray's neighbours vacated a room for me. The nights were still cool and, despite my protests, my host provided me with a large quilt although I was sure that someone else would have sorely missed it that night.

At about five in the morning, as dawn broke, I got up and sat outside watching the women in the village silently come out of their homes, brushes in hand. They started to sweep up the remains of straw scattered the previous night for their goats and cattle. They made a small bonfire so that their children could warm their stiff cold limbs as soon as they were awake. As the flames died down, the hot ashes were scraped out and their heat used to boil water for an early morning drink.

Manojma's routine consisted entirely of household chores, caring for the children and sleeping, while her husband's was dictated by the seasons, and whether or not there was work. In spring Ramashray worked in two shifts, both four hours long. In the middle of the day he returned home for lunch and a rest. His second shift ended as darkness fell and Manojma waited to feed him before feeding herself. He went to sleep as soon as he had eaten. He told me that he went to sleep under the stars in the hot months.

I observed that there could be no privacy in their lives. Everything had to be discussed in the open. My interpreter told me that when they wanted to make love they had to go into the fields when it was dark. Yet Hindus are fastidious, prudish and discreet, and the lack of privacy is particularly hard for the women during menstruation. Manojma saved any bits of rag she could lay her hands on and used torn pieces of old clothes.

In their community, a father often starts to look for a suitable husband for his daughter before her periods start. This is, in part, to protect the pubescent girls from harassment by bullish landlords. However, the time to think of marriage for Tetri would depend on when they could raise some money for her dowry. They expected to have to pay 3,000 rupees, double her father's annual earnings, so it was most likely to be when Manoj married and his bride brought her dowry. Ramashray sadly acknowledged that the choice of Tetri's husband would depend more on what his family would accept as a dowry than on the quality of his human characteristics. When a boy had been found and the dowry accepted, they would proceed immediately. The rituals would be kept very simple. If Tetri was still under thirteen, she would stay with her parents after the ceremony, maybe for another two or three years. As soon as she was menstruating regularly, her father would send word to her in-laws before taking her to her young husband. The young girls who played in the village and who were already married could be identified by the red powder they wore in their hair parting.

For the time being, Tetri had taken to caring for little Kishan, and during my visits to Dighi I noticed how well the small boy coped. His sister taught him how to feed himself and he became very mobile in and around the vicinity of his own home. He used his toes like fingers, to feel his way. Sometimes he played with an empty blue plastic bottle, an old tractor bolt, and a strip of iron, half of a broken hinge for a heavy door. He amused himself for a long time with these three simple objects, experimenting with the different noises he could make. He continually felt for and touched his sister's and brothers' faces, mouths and ears, hugging them and covering them with kisses, although this show of affection irritated his twin. Every now and then Kishan pleaded with his father to take him to Patna, for he was convinced that people in a big city would be able to make his eyes better.

His mother steadfastly believed he had the power to see again. He just had some cloudy skin which had grown over the front of his pupils. If that could be removed he would have his sight back. After all, he seemed still to respond when she shone a lamp in front of him. 'He doesn't actually say he can see the light but I can see some contraction. If the sight were gone for ever this wouldn't happen, the eyes would be dead and motionless. But they aren't, they aren't. Sometimes when I look at him, even if he's smiling, I feel overwhelmed with a kind of depression. I feel quite inadequate not knowing what to do about it and the worry goes round and around inside my head. Maybe he's blind because of something I or Ramashray have done wrong. But why should he be the one to suffer? He's too young to have been really bad. I just don't know.'

'It's the worst thing that has ever happened to us,' interrupted Ramashray. 'It would have been better if Kishan had died. This we both could have accepted. Now I just worry about his future. He is going to be a burden on someone for the rest of his life.' He hung his head sadly. He didn't have the same optimism as his wife that Kishan could see again.

On the days when there was no work he would often sit outside his home, smoking bidis, chewing tobacco and pondering the situation. 'I find myself thinking about the children's future, not what they will do but if there is any real future for them and Kishan's eyes and the burden of the loan I have to repay – and often sitting here I find that all the difficulties of life seem just too much to bear. When I'm

161

hungry as well it is difficult to explain exactly how I feel. Just very weak and wrecked from inside. Sometimes I repent ever having been born. I get fed up wondering why I've been born in this place where there isn't enough work.

'In many ways I think I'm a bit of a loner. I don't get too involved emotionally with other people living in my neighbourhood. Let's say I keep at arm's distance, but I am friendly and generally there is good feeling there. I've got a secret plan, though. I'm going to organise a certificate for myself with my age marked down saying I'm under thirty-five. Then I'll be able to get a good job in government or some work in a factory. I don't mind what it is or how hard I have to labour. Anything to get away from all this.'

He was curious about the world beyond the constraints imposed on him by his financial instability. 'I like stopping by a friend's house and listening to the radio, the local news and some music, but it can be quite difficult to hear what is going on because someone is usually talking all the time. Sometimes I go on impulse to the cinema in Hajipur and watch a Hindi movie, but always on my own. I don't really have any heroes because I can't afford to go very often.'

Ramashray shook his head when I asked him if he ever lost his temper. 'I'm not a violent person and not the kind to get caught up in a fight with someone, but if anybody ever hit my wife I think I would kill them myself, just like that, with my own hands. I get angry sometimes and Manojma and I do quarrel, but that's normal, isn't it? It usually happens when she yells at me when I don't have money and she has no food to cook. I get cross with Manoj when he won't go to school, and sometimes I even get angry with an imaginary person when I don't get work. Although I do get very frustrated, I'm not an envious person. I accept, on the whole, the way things are. I'm just not lucky, which is why I'm hungry. Still, I seem to have adjusted.'

Manojma cried when her husband quarrelled with her. 'It's not unusual for Ramashray to beat me, but I know the little ones' crying for food irritates him. He thinks it's his fault, not being able to provide for us, but of course I know it isn't. The happiest time of my life was before I married. I had no worries. Not a care in the world. I remember my father feeling really pleased when he found Ramashray for me with his fine looks and good brain. He's very handsome, don't you think? It's not his fault the way things have turned out for us. I'm quite satisfied with him but not with the life we've had together. Why has it been like this? Why? Why? Why? This continual battle of trying to hold everything together defeats me sometimes.'

One day when I arrived in the village after a few weeks' absence Manojma stood huddled by her front door. Her face registered no look of welcome or surprise when she saw me – she just put her hand to her stomach. I thought that she must be ill, maybe with the monthly cramps. Tetri was sitting by her mother's feet, as if frozen. Where was Ramashray? Manoj gestured across the roadway: 'He's in discussion with some other men.' Manojma called out to him. Ramashray crossed over towards his house. His mouth was puckered and his eyes looked stern.

'What is happening?' I asked.

'I've been working in the fields for five days without pay,' he sighed. 'Yesterday evening we were told the landlord had no money. If he had the money of course he would pay us, but he was waiting to receive his pension from the railways. It would come through soon, he wasn't quite sure when, but he couldn't pay any of us now. I have no more money myself now, nothing with which to buy any rice or gram. None of us has eaten for two days and I don't know how I'm going to get any rupees to buy food until later next week.'

The children were gazing at their father as he spoke, their small faces pleading.

'How can we get by for another five days, and it's so cold at night too. I'll have to try and get some rice on credit.'

Ramashray swallowed his pride as I pulled two 10-rupee notes out of my wallet and sent Manoj off to the store. Manojma broke up a few twigs and started a small fire in preparation for cooking her family their first meal for three days – boiled rice with a little dal. Half an hour later Ramashray crouched down inside the front room, the children sitting on the small wooden blocks as they ate together from the same large plate, hungrily scooping up the steaming substance in their fingers, gulping it down in silence. Manojma scraped the bottom of the pot, making sure that nothing was wasted but keeping just a little back for herself. She would eat when her children had filled their bellies.

I waited outside and rested my camera case on the ground, turning my head away in embarrassment at being a spectator in such a situation. As I looked down, my eyes rested on the black leather bag and I winced when I thought of all the expensive equipment I was carrying with me. On the return train journey to Delhi I met my mother by prior arrangement in Benares. We travelled in air-conditioned comfort and at Lucknow the train stopped for half an hour during which time dinner was served. I left the carriage for a while to purchase some magazines and some fruit. Shortly after the train had pulled out of the station I checked that all my luggage was in its place. The camera case wasn't there. A young boy perched on the opposite top berth recalled someone picking it up but he couldn't remember who. I sat down in a daze, then puzzled at my uncharacteristic foresight. I had packed all my exposed rolls of film in my overnight bag which was now under my feet. I thought of the aggravation ahead – finding a police station, where I would have to file a report; filling in insurance claim forms; getting hold of another camera – and then I thought of the pride of a hungry man who wouldn't ask me for money to help feed his children. I felt humbled and slightly stupid that I had so carelessly left my equipment unattended in a busy railway terminus.

8

A Middle-class Family
in Delhi

The atmosphere in India's capital, New Delhi, evokes in me a variety of ambivalent responses. On my first visit I found it a glorious city and I loved to walk along the fine wide tree-lined avenues, past the spacious colonial-style bungalows, marvelling at the immaculate gardens and sprawling well-watered lawns. I was overawed by the majesty of the parliament buildings designed by Britain's foremost turn-of-the-century architect, Sir Edwin Lutyens. They are built of pale pink stone imported from neighbouring Rajasthan, and are approached by the splendid mile-and-a-half-long Raj Path. On subsequent visits I would take my son to swim at one of the innumerable luxurious five-star hotels where there were expensive restaurants offering exotic oriental cuisines, and shops and boutiques selling a wide variety of silverware, antiquities, gorgeous silks and the softest Kashmiri woollens. The cultural events staged in the city are comparable to most Western capitals. There are theatres, auditoriums, where every evening one can watch the finest classical Indian dance, art galleries and museums, and also many cinemas, yet though India boasts the largest movie industry in the world the standard of film projection and sound is paradoxically extremely poor. However, despite the city's excellent facilities, I began to find that it lacked the soul and Indian-ness to be found in other major cities.

165

New Delhi was developed by the British as a new seat of parliament and the centre for their troops, its position chosen as being more central than Calcutta in the east, the former seat of Imperial rule. The adjoining city of Old Delhi with its bustling markets has never lost its thrill for me, but for centuries it has been an overcrowded and congested place, so the site chosen for the new capital was the land to the south, a flat plain interspersed with gardens and many fine ruins of Mughal tombs and monuments.

Since Independence in 1947, New Delhi has been a city inhabited by those families displaced during Partition. The contemporary middle-class Delhi-wallah, so named by other Indians in mocking contempt, enjoys one of the best living standards in the East. Throughout the suburbs of the city, leafy residential enclaves have been constructed, designed around communal gardens, each having its own shopping centre, with a bakery, vegetable stall, cobbler, hardware store, stationer, general grocery, news-stand – every imaginable daily need catered for. They also have their own English-language schools, libraries, banks and taxi and motor-rickshaw stands.

Despite industrial growth, the lower middle classes and workers of Delhi have fared less well. Property prices have doubled since Indira Gandhi's assassination and the continuing unrest in the Punjab, which have forced many Punjabi Hindus to sell their properties and invest in the capital.

As new industries have been developed so too have homes for workers and executives. Many of these are in neighbouring Uttar Pradesh, on the far side of the Jumna River which flows to the east of the city. Great incentives have been offered by the local government, encouragements to both large- and small-scale industrialists to invest and settle here. There are innumerable electronics factories where TVs and radios are constructed, factories making engineering components and food and drugs, and some textile plants. Other 'trans-Jumna' colonies sprang up during the 1977 State of Emergency when Sanjay Gandhi, in an effort to clear up the old city, bulldozed slum areas and forcibly resettled the slum-dwellers in suburbs such as Seemapuri, installing entire families in one-roomed apartments overlooking a shared courtyard. There were no toilet facilities and an outdoor tap was often shared by up to five hundred people, causing continual friction and tension. Such places are now bursting, housing anything from twenty to fifty thousand people. While they were being constructed, the developers sieved off large amounts of government funds for themselves, failing to put in proper drainage so that the air is now pervaded with the smell of stagnant water and human excrement. At the outset these dwellings were not allotted caste-wise, so in one block there could be both Brahmins and Harijans. Social habits die hard and there has been constant bickering and little unity. Some people have extended their houses by building a room on top, renting this out to augment their income, thus causing more frustration with further overcrowding. Rents can be as high as 300 rupees a month for such a room, which has no facilities except four walls and a roof which invariably leaks during the monsoon periods.

In an attempt to combat overcrowding in the city centre the Delhi Development Association was inaugurated. Its original intention was to provide homes for people with education and qualifications who, although their income was low, could afford a deposit and mortgage payments. Unfortunately, corruption among contractors has resulted in inefficiently erected buildings, where poorly construc-ted walls and ceilings have been known to collapse, but as the scheme is supported by the government it is almost impossible to take those responsible to court. The complexes were designed with neither imagination nor sympathy for those who would inhabit them. 'Architecture' was a borrowed concept, and what was built mirrored European development after the Second World War, with no regard paid to the climatic conditions of the country. Families are cooped up in cramped rooms with minimal facilities. The ethics inherent in traditional communities have been lost, and within the vicinity of these new colonies mugging and vandalism are daily events. There are large boards promising parks and trees, few of which have materialised. Local medical facilities are quite insuffi-cient – one doctor may visit a nearby surgery once a month and then have less than a minute to see each patient. However, in a city where many sleep in the streets, bearable during the hot weather but miserable in the winter when night temperatures some-times drop to near freezing, housing is at a premium. Everyone offered a flat will jump at the opportunity to have a home of their own.

Fortunately during the months when I was conducting my research I was able to afford the rent of a large and comfortable flat close to the diplomatic enclaves. My landlord was a Rajput who had worked in the Indian Civil Service and I observed that after an active professional life he was enjoying a comfortable retirement. His son had studied accountancy and was living in Canada and his daughter was married to a lawyer who practised in Calcutta. To have a career in the ICS is one of the most popular ambitions for all those fortunate enough to have secured a decent education. In addition to the possibility of job satisfaction, in a country which is unable to afford social security and basic health care government employees are offered stability, a decent wage, a pension and, moreover, subsidised rented accommodation at the outset in apartments which are far superior to those provided in the haphazard and dilapidated modern schemes of the DDA.

For my final piece of research I wanted to talk to a young man working for the government, someone who belonged to an urban group of professionals whose families were beginning to enjoy the recent surge in social and economic standards of living. After Bihar, I was a little weary of despair and hoped to talk to people whose out-look on life was less encumbered by unending struggle. I wanted to meet a family who felt themselves to be a part of an independent India moving towards the twenty-first century, where positive change for a better life was a real possibility. My journalist friend in Patna gave me an introduction to a colleague working in his Delhi headquarters. There I met a young female receptionist whose name was Latha, and she told me that Sridhar, her husband, worked in the Ministry of Finance. If I wished I could come and meet her family the following weekend. They lived with their two small children in a second-floor flat of a housing complex situated within walking distance of her husband's office in Parliament Square.

It was a large estate, nearly half a mile in length, each four-storey block of flats painted red and yellow. On a Sunday morning in early December there was a relaxed and convivial atmosphere on the stretches of parched grass which ran between the tenements. Charpoys had been brought out for the elderly to sit on, to read the

33 Ramashray and his family in front of the house his father built   34 The monsoon rains have finally arrived   35 Thirty-year-old Manojma is prematurely aged by poverty and hardship   36 Tetri with her father

newspapers and chat in the shade of the pawpaw trees, while small children played on their bikes and the older ones played cricket. A cobbler stitched and polished. A middle-aged gentleman soaped himself at the handpump, amidst washing lines hung with drying dhotis, saris and sheets billowing in a warm breeze. The istri-wallah, one of a branch of the Dhobi caste, had set up a table where he pressed the dry garments with a heavy metal iron heated with hot coals. Sacred cows nibbled at the scorched turf, and tradesmen plied their wares, their bicycles piled high with rope, pots and pans and other ironmongery goods. The tenants were of various religious denominations. Hindus, Muslims, Sikhs and Christians lived side by side, sharing staircases and rubbish dumps with little friction. Within such urban communities, where the inhabitants enjoy financial stability, caste consciousness has begun to evaporate.

A few months earlier, Sridhar had suggested to his wife that her mother should move in with them. As she was the eldest person present, out of courtesy on my first visit I asked Mrs Gopal to provide me with some background information and details of her grandchildren's routine. Before I had a chance to talk to the rest of the family she seemed anxious to recount to me the trauma which had preceded her son-in-law's invitation. She was sitting on the edge of the couch feeding her granddaughter, and she began talking in excited bursts about the events surrounding the birth of the little girl.

'It happened during a Saturday night just over a year ago and I was still living in my old home. As it was Diwali I decided to make some special sweets and bring them here for my grandson, Deepak, who was three years old at the time. Also I had prepared Latha's favourite dish, a potato curry. I worked quite late in the kitchen that evening. When finally I went to bed I found I couldn't get to sleep, perhaps from overexertion. I was just drifting off when I heard knocking at the door. I didn't open it. Being all on my own I couldn't just let anyone in at that time and I couldn't hear who it was. Then I heard Sridhar shouting, "Mummy, Mummy, it's me. You must come." When I opened the door he told me that Latha was in a serious condition. She was bleeding very heavily. She was pregnant at the time but the baby wasn't due for another six weeks. He'd come on his motorbike but at my suggestion we took a taxi from the local

37 Sridhar and Latha's arranged marriage has brought happiness and stability for their children and for Latha's mother as well as for themselves

stand back to his flat because we'd never have been able to find one in the middle of the night near their home. I took some money with me too, rupees which I hid in a secret place. Even in an emergency nobody will do anything for you unless you can hand over cash. As I entered their flat I saw Latha leaning against the kitchen door in a dazed state, standing in a pool of blood. Fortunately Deepak was still fast asleep so I tore the sheet off their bed, and wrapped it tightly around Latha in an attempt to stop the flow. Then we woke up the little boy and all went straight to the hospital. The nurses there could see Latha was in a very bad way but before she was taken to the emergency unit formalities had to be completed and reassurances given that all costs would be met. We were told that the bleeding couldn't be stopped, nor could they hear a heartbeat, so they didn't think they could save the child although they would do all they could to save the mother. The doctor looked accusingly at Sridhar, suggesting that maybe he and Latha had been doing something they shouldn't have at such an advanced stage in pregnancy. Something must have started off the heavy bleeding. She would have to have a caesarean but they needed more blood, so Sridhar was given a sample for the correct blood group and sent to fetch a supply from the nearest blood bank. There's one in Connaught Circus which stays open twenty-four hours a day. He came back with three bottles, each costing a hundred and eighty rupees, and immediately the blood was given to Latha. However, when they started to empty the third bottle she began to react badly and Sridhar had to go off again into the night. While all this was going on I was sitting in the hospital lobby. Deepak was lying on my lap, sleeping. I felt very frightened. As it began to get light, we were told the baby had been born, but she was very frail and had been placed in an incubator on another floor. But we were so worried about Latha that we hardly thought about the child. It seemed too unreal.

'By seven in the morning Latha showed signs of improvement but her breathing was light and for another three hours an oxygen mask was placed over her face. Sridhar took Deepak back home and I sat at the foot of her bed. At around lunchtime she opened her eyes. "Have I got a child?" she asked. "Yes, yes," I said. "You have got a beautiful girl," I reassured her, although at the time I hadn't set eyes on the baby. She seemed pleased and satisfied that the child was alive although I don't think she really believed me. She was barely conscious and soon drifted off to sleep.'

At that moment Latha came with two cups of cardamom-flavoured tea and I looked at the child who was trying to climb off the couch – a beautiful, chubby, healthy little girl.

'I was sure I was going to die,' interrupted Latha, delighted to fill me in with more grisly details. 'When I started to bleed I got very panicky. I thought I wasn't going to be around for much longer. It was strange because I had no pain at all, no sign of being in labour. They told me that the placenta had broken away, causing a lesion in a blood vessel.'

'Before being discharged from the hospital the doctors told Latha she could have another child if she wanted one,' Mrs Gopal continued, 'but we know a third child is difficult. It is so expensive – the hospital charges alone amounted to seven thousand rupees. Better to curtail now that one has a good family with a girl and a boy. To my mind that should be sufficient for them. Being born is just the start of this very long journey called life.'

Mrs Gopal spoke from experience. Ever since she left home to get married herself, she had constantly overcome difficulties and crossed hurdles – hazards she had encountered through no fault of her own. Her father was a clerk in the Kerala High Court. The family were Brahmins, orthodox Shivites, and although they were unable to enjoy luxuries there was enough to pay for a decent education and for her to qualify as a stenographer. Marriage with a young man whose family were employed by a large petroleum company in Bombay at the time appeared suitable – and so it was for a few years, until the breadwinners were made redundant.

Mrs Gopal was reluctant to expand on the reasons for the breakdown in her marriage – 'My family situation went "out of gear",' she explained – but she suffered both physical and mental torture for a number of years. She couldn't return to her village because of the shame and embarrassment she would have brought to the family. Her parents wrote to her elder brother who had settled in Delhi. Fortunately he agreed to let her live with his family. His wife would look after the two little girls and Mrs Gopal could look for work.

'I was fully at his courtesy, an uncomfortable situation, but with my daughters to care for I had no choice. He found me a typing job with a salary of three hundred rupees a month – half of this I gave him for living expenses, the remainder paid for the children's education. It was difficult but better than staying with a man who was both an impossible husband and a hopeless father.

'Two months after I started working I fell ill with an infected gland in my neck. I was so frightened and worried. What if I didn't get better? What would happen to the children? Their father wasn't capable of looking after them and even if he could he wouldn't have wanted to. I prayed and prayed to God to give me back my good health. It turned out to be TB and fortunately, after a course of injections which my good brother kindly paid for, the swelling subsided.'

'My father discovered where we were,' remembered Latha, 'and occasionally he would visit us. There were dreadful rows. He was always asking Mummy for money. I haven't seen him for over fifteen years. We don't even know where he is now. I don't like him but I rarely think about him. In fact I don't even care if he's dead or alive.' Her mother frowned at her. She didn't like this kind of talk. She believed that her husband was not a bad man and that his weakness of character and inability to accept responsibility was the result of childhood trauma.

Life in Delhi had settled into a steady routine. Latha and her younger sister attended Tamil-language schools, and then spent three years in college, and Mrs Gopal continued in her typing job, working hard and devoting her life to giving them the chances and privileges she had been unable to enjoy.

'Mummy was a very loving person, but with a temper too. Often she would beat us over quite trivial matters,' laughed Latha.

'My only wish was for the children to be properly married so I had to ensure they developed good characters,' retorted her mother. Tradition dictated a husband from the same community and Mrs Gopal discovered that because of her background no prospective husband would come forward for her daughters. 'It doesn't look good if one hasn't been kept by one's own husband. They would never accept that maybe he was at fault; the woman must always take the blame. Even if a man is a crook or a drunkard, he is never in the wrong.'

Sridhar, a Tamil Brahmin, was brought to their attention by a mutual friend. First Mrs Gopal met his grandmother and she told her all the family history. If they were prepared to accept Latha from such a background, all would be well. That was her precondition. Every day in the newspapers there were reports of the deaths of young brides. Greedy parents would burn alive their son's new wife if funds did not arrive as prearranged. A young girl in a middle-class home would be doused in kerosene and set alight, her in-laws claiming her sari had caught fire in a kitchen accident. Any kind of harassment was to be avoided. Mrs Gopal was adamant that no man should ever treat either of her daughters badly. An added enhancement to Sridhar's suitability as a husband was that neither of his parents was alive, thus he was left with few responsibilities.

When Latha became officially engaged to Sridhar she had not met him. 'As soon as Mummy had seen him and liked him, then I said "Okay". We knew that whatever happened was for our benefit. That was how we were brought up. When I first met him I thought, goodness, he really is stupid. He looked so scruffy and my sister said I should refuse him. Then I thought I should not just say no because of the way he looked and Mummy pointed out that he only looked bad because no one was looking after him.'

'I think even now she still thinks I'm not very bright!' interrupted Sridhar. To me, he seemed an intelligent man with an amiable character.

'If I had some photographs I could show you how dreadful he looked, all puny and pale. No one would have guessed that he was thirty years old. He didn't eat properly and spent all his spare time going to the movies. We really took him in hand and smartened him up.'

Given their modest means, their wedding, a once-in-a-lifetime celebration, was a colourful and extravagant affair, but in comparison to the Marwaris' wedding in Bombay there was none of the vulgar display of wealth; the emphasis was on the religious and ritualistic implications of marriage. The bride and her mother wore their finest silk saris, but their jewellery was coloured metal and paste diamond.

The groom and his brother were simply swathed in yards of stiff beige cotton, leaving their arms and shoulders naked. There was no ornate mandapan, and the ceremony and rites were conducted on a raised platform covered with handwoven cotton durries. Instead of there being a lavish feast, the guests queued to be seated at long trestle tables and were served by a team of specially hired Brahmin cooks who ladled from tin buckets the traditional South Indian dishes of rice served on a banana leaf and a variety of vegetables and pickles.

After the marriage they adjusted well to one another, they told me, although Sridhar was surprised to find he had married a girl with a very quick temper.

'I do get very cross,' admitted Latha, 'but once I have given vent to my anger it is all over. We do have our differences but we're together for life so we may as well overcome them. In these arranged marriages one makes oneself adapt to the partner and nine times out of ten it works. I know I am lucky. My husband has a very good nature and he is a considerate man too.' After ten years they said they fought a lot, both having strong characters, but they also showed each other a great deal of affection. They enjoyed teasing each other, and kissed and cuddled quite openly in front of me. Having both come from backgrounds where hardships had had to be overcome, they were content with what they had achieved for themselves and were now reserving their ambitions for their children.

Their living quarters were very compact and on entering the first time I found the smallness and darkness overwhelming. The front door opened directly into a tiny living-cum-bedroom, dominated by a large colour television set which was placed in the corner behind the door. There was a two-seater bench, a large single bed on which Mrs Gopal slept with her grandson, and two armchairs made from wood and cane. From the living room a door led to an open area where they ate off mats on the floor. In here were two large refrigerators, locked cupboards, a sewing machine, an air-cooler and another door opening on to a balcony. There was a small kitchen with running water and two calor gas cookers. The only proper bedroom, shared by Sridhar, Latha and their baby daughter, was entirely filled by a double bed. The WC was Indian style – an opening in the floor lined with a ceramic basin – and in the wash room stood a large plastic bucket which they filled with water, using a small jug to take a shower. The water supply was erratic. The tanks on the top of the block of flats were filled in the late afternoon and by early morning they were empty.

The flat was crammed with furniture, most of which was crudely built but practical. When Mrs Gopal came to live with them she brought all her possessions. She said she liked to keep the flat spotless but where food was prepared and where they washed were first priority. The walls were in fact badly stained, and everywhere Deepak had scribbled in pencil and crayon. Dust had collected on the cupboards and shelves where gifts from friends were displayed. However, they lacked for nothing in the way of luxuries. They were not interested in watching Hindi movies so had no desire to own a video but Sridhar had a large collection of tapes: Hindi and Tamil music and a little Western pop. Decorations in the flat were minimal – a few religious posters and some glossy photographs of alpine scenes. The floor was made of polished chipped marble, commonly used as it was cheap, easy to wash and cool in summer. There were overhead fans in the living room and bedroom and on cold winter nights they used electric heaters. They did not mind that there was no air-conditioning. Purchase and running costs apart, they all spent the hottest hours of the day working in air-conditioned offices.

Sridhar's job entitled him to 500 rupees a month for a flat, to which he added a further 35 rupees. Gas and electricity came to approximately 120 rupees. They shared a maid with six other families. While they were at work she spent an hour cleaning the floors and washing dishes for which she was paid 80 rupees a month. A sweeper was supposed to come to clean the toilet but Latha complained that he only came once a month when he wanted money. 'Two days before he's due for payment he comes around all friendly with his "Namastes" [Good day] and "How are you, Madam?"'

A graduate in commerce from Delhi University, Sridhar worked in the government department which controlled all state-owned banks, the Department of Economic Affairs. He was responsible for collecting and circulating all relevant information between them and compiling their annual report. 'All the sections of our office give me their "year end" activities and I compile information which is then published in book form and circulated throughout all government departments and state banks.'

Nearly every month he travelled outside the city, attending financial conferences and meetings. He was a part of the vast bureaucratic empire inherited from the British, a small cog in a big old-fashioned wheel from which India was slowly emerging. When he travelled he flew or went by rail, first class, and stayed in air-conditioned comfort courtesy of the government, although when the family made their annual trip to South India to visit relatives they made the thirty-six-hour train journey in a second-class carriage. He was paid a monthly salary of 2,200 rupees in addition to his rent allowance, and health and pension insurance. He did not find his work stretched his intellectual capacities but was happy for the financial stability provided, a covetable position in India. Before marriage he was an enthusiastic reader, wrote short stories in Tamil for pleasure and saw every serious movie presented in town. Spare time was spent with his friends, shooting and editing their own films. He rarely socialised with girls unless in company and only put himself forward for marriage at his younger brother's suggestion. His brother had wanted to find a wife for himself and tradition dictated that the elder son should marry first. By nature, Sridhar was serious and thoughtful rather than outgoing, content to devote himself to the needs of his children and wife. He lacked the ostentation and materialistic pretensions so prevalent today among his city peers and was doubtful and suspicious of those currently responsible for the running of the country. He was a great admirer of the former socialist leader Morarji Desai, believing that the destiny of the country would have been quite different if he had taken the leadership of the Congress party at the time Indira Gandhi came to power. 'He had good principles and he stuck to them. It was disunity among his colleagues that brought his downfall.' Sridhar now felt a mixture of pessimism for India but optimism for his own children's future. 'This country will only move forward if it can find a way of blending all that is best in our traditions and make generally available a decent education and basic health care. Only in this way will the evils of caste prejudice be eradicated. We should be ashamed that nearly half our population does not have clean water to drink.'

Latha worked full-time for the newspaper, a radical publication whose head office was based in Calcutta. A senior colleague spoke about her in affectionate terms, admiring her spirit of goodwill and her sincere character. 'She looks after all the incoming and outgoing mail, the office telephones, booking calls and taking messages and organising our expenses and tickets for travel. She handles her diverse responsibilities with great efficiency. The prevailing impression is of her constantly besieged with work because it is a small office, heavily overstaffed by journalists and advertising personnel. Everyone leans on her because the office babu is a cantankerous old man, best avoided. She despatches all the articles to headquarters by air-packet every day, checking through them beforehand so they can be counter-checked on arrival. If she was at all careless one of our articles could be mislaid. Her smiling face is the first thing one sees as one opens the office door and even when she's burdened down with work she is always willing to be helpful.'

Her mother still worked as a stenographer in the central offices of GEM, one of India's largest manufacturing concerns, a job she had had for nearly twenty-five years. They were each paid 1,600 rupees a month – about £20 for a forty-hour week in a country where the cost of living is approximately half that of a European city. Between them they took it in turns to take Deepak to a cathedral nursery school and leave Varsha at the crèche where she had been cared for during the daytime since she was four months old.

Mrs Gopal worried that the children lacked the constant affection they needed for their emotional development, but their parents were ambitious for them in other ways, wanting them to have the best education available, and to study in Hindi, English and their native Tamil. At least two wages would be necessary to afford the fees. When I suggested that maybe their grandmother could stay at home with them, Mrs Gopal shook her head. 'I don't want to be a burden on anyone. I insist on paying my own way. I am sure, too, that if I stopped working my brain would become idle – I may even become mentally disturbed. But I am devoted to the little ones. They are so much a part of me – it is as if they were my own son and daughter.'

They invited me to come and share an evening meal with them. When I arrived Latha was lying back on the living-room bed while her mother was preparing the dinner. This was her time of the month, she explained with a smile, showing no trace of embarrassment. She was not allowed into the kitchen for three days. Before her mother came to live with them she was unable to be particular about keeping herself segregated, but now she was happy to take a break. Tomorrow, the fourth day, she would go into the shower room and take a ceremonial wash before re-entering the kitchen. She knew too that without her mother's help they would not be able to mind the children. When they came home from the office, tired out, it was the old lady who helped Deepak with his homework and played cricket with him while he entertained the fantasy that he was the captain of the national team.

'Mummy's a very great lady for overcoming so successfully all the problems she has encountered. Now that life has sorted itself out she has become a very dear person. She wouldn't hurt a fly. We never leave her alone now. Everywhere we go, she comes too.'

Mealtimes were important family occasions. None of them ever ate alone. Latha and her mother shared the cooking and Sridhar helped to peel potatoes and vegetables and gave Varsha her bottle. Apart from being responsible for purchasing the food – fresh vegetables from a local market, and rice and sugar from the wholesaler – he took an active interest in all household matters. They enjoyed eating and the preparation of food was undertaken with great care. In the home they were strictly vegetarian, and used neither garlic nor eggs, although they were not worried about sharing their food with other castes. They ate a variety of South Indian fare, usually three different vegetable dishes for their evening meal with chapattis, rice and dal. But Sridhar said that when he was away on his business travels he sometimes ate meat and occasionally drank a bottle of beer.

They were practising Hindus although the fundamental beliefs in no way dominated their approach to life. Quite simply, as a matter of habit, they maintained certain rituals and observed their own community's major festivals, believing there was stability and an inherent value in honouring the basic traditions of their faith. After her birth, Varsha's horoscope was read by computer, but the reading was so complex and full of information that they doubted whether all that was forecast could be achieved in one lifetime.

While his wife was adamant that it didn't exist, Sridhar neither believed nor disbelieved in rebirth. There was nothing to prove its existence to him, as he had never met anybody who could remember a former life. But to Mrs Gopal, the idea of the life cycle had a special meaning – the eternity of the soul. When the body grew old, one changed into fresh clothing and entered a new form. Every morning, while the rest of the family were still asleep, she performed puja. She believed that because of her devotion the gods had rewarded her with healthy grandchildren and peace of mind. All she ever wanted was to see her daughters happily settled. When death came, it would be welcome.

Latha prayed sometimes, but unlike her mother she did not remember the gods every day. More important to her was not how often one said one's prayers but one's social behaviour. 'Your friends should be true to you and not say bullshit things behind your back. It is a person's good character which is important, not his caste and creed.'

I did not spend a great deal of time with Sridhar and his family. They worked hard every day and were tired in the evenings when they arrived home. Most weekends they would see their relations or friends and when they were all together they chatted with each other in their native tongue. As they spoke English there was no point in me asking an interpreter to accompany us so of course the only information I could gather was what they intended me to hear. Hence it was only possible for me to make some general assumptions regarding their characters. Outwardly their lives did not appear in any way out of the ordinary yet I found Sridhar and Latha were unrepresentative of the majority of contemporary middle class society. Western bourgeois values have recently penetrated Indian urban society, replacing the old ways of graciousness and hospitality. I was enchanted to meet two young people who attached greater importance to spiritual and social values than to saving up for a new Maruti car, and who considered it not only their duty but their pleasure to care for the older generation.

Marriage in India is a constant to be relied upon, not the brittle framework it has become in the West today, and while Sridhar and Latha's personal contentment and lack of personal ambition may appear to us to have made their lives unremarkable, a steady job, good family relationships and healthy children are at a premium in the world's largest democracy and tragically only within the grasp of a small minority. Fortunately Sridhar and Latha were grateful to be a part of that minority.

After many visits to India I have often reflected on what compelled me to keep on returning. Gregarious by nature, I admired people's graciousness and warm spirits and the pleasure taken in moments shared. Relaxation and the goodness of the soul was their code, and there was a lack of the aggression so prevalent in the West. I was always riveted by their attention to each simple act. For instance, the manner in which a bootcleaner applied the polish to one's shoes, and then made them shine, was for him a work of art. The Indian people seemed to have a great sense of humour and delight in the absurd. Once the business of keeping body and soul together had been overcome, their main aim in life was to enjoy themselves. It was these qualities which remained uppermost in my mind and which make me look forward each time to going back.

Bibliography

Akbar, M. J., *India: The Siege Within*, Harmondsworth: Penguin, 1985

Basham, A. L., *The Wonder That Was India*, London: William Collins, 1954

Cameron, James, *An Indian Summer*, London: Macmillan, 1974

Campbell, Joseph, *The Masks of God: Oriental Mythology*, New York: Viking, 1962

Cassen, R. H., *India: Population, Economy, Society*, London: Macmillan, 1978

Chaudhuri, Nirad C., *Hinduism: A Religion to Live By*, London: Chatto & Windus, 1979

Collins, Larry, and Lapierre, Dominique, *Freedom at Midnight*, Delhi: Vikas Publishing, 1976

Dubois, Abbé J. A., *Hindu Manners, Customs and Ceremonies*, Delhi: Oxford University Press, 1906

Dumont, Louis, *Homo Hierarchicus: The Caste System and Its Implications*, Paris: Editions Gallimard, 1966

Fishlock, Trevor, *India File*, London: John Murray, 1985

Freeman, James M., *Untouchable: An Indian Life History*, London: George Allen & Unwin, 1979

Hiro, Dilip, *Inside India Today*, London: Routledge & Kegan Paul, 1976

Hobson, Sarah, *Family Web: A Story of India*, London: John Murray, 1978

Hutton, J. H., *Caste in India*, Bombay: Oxford University Press, 1946

Keay, John, *Into India*, London: John Murray, 1973

Kung, Hans, *Christianity and the World Religions*, London: William Collins, 1987

Lannoy, Richard, *The Speaking Tree: A Study of Indian Culture and Society*, London: Oxford University Press, 1971

181

Bibliography

Lapierre, Dominique, *City of Joy*, London: Century Hutchinson, 1986

Marriott, McKim (ed.), *Village India: Studies in the Little Community*, Chicago: University of Chicago Press, 1955

Mehta, Ved, *Mahatma Gandhi: and His Apostles*, London: André Deutsch, 1977

Moorhouse, Geoffrey, *Calcutta: The City Revealed*, London: Weidenfeld & Nicholson, 1971

Naipaul, V. S., *An Area of Darkness*, London: André Deutsch, 1964

——*A Wounded Civilisation*, London: André Deutsch, 1977

O'Flaherty, Wendy (trans.), *The Rig Veda*, Harmondsworth: Penguin, 1981

Radice, Betty (ed.), *Hindu Myths*, Harmondsworth: Penguin, 1975

Rice, Edward, *Eastern Definitions*, New York: Doubleday, 1980

Roy, Manisha, *Bengali Women*, Chicago: University of Chicago Press, 1972

Spear, Percival, *A History of India*, Vol. 2, Harmondsworth: Penguin, 1965

Thapar, Romila, *A History of India*, Vol. 1, Harmondsworth: Penguin, 1966

Tod, James, *Annals and Antiquities of Rajasthan*, Vols 1 & 2, London: Routledge & Kegan Paul, 1914

Wilson, John, *Indian Caste*, Vols 1 & 2, Delhi: KK Book Distributors, 1877

Zinkin, Taya, *India*, London: Oxford University Press, 1964

Acknowledgments

Throughout the period of my research I encountered great warmth, generosity and the hospitality for which Indians are legend. It would be impossible for me to list here all those who gave freely of their help and time, and the following are remembered for having extended kindnesses beyond the boundaries of anyone's expectation: Vinu Baig, Dr Gladys Indra, Freddie Favre, Bunny Page, K.M. and Meera Kishan, Beena and Kasturi Khaitan, Maan Kanwaar, Geetha Reddy, all the families portrayed in this book, and especially Yuburaj Ghimire.

Patricia Lankester and Michael Yorke patiently read through the first draft and gave me their much valued criticism and opinion.

Tony Colwell, my editor at Jonathan Cape, has been unstintingly and painstakingly persistent in criticism and encouragement, along with Annelise Evans and Elizabeth Smith of the editorial department.

I am deeply grateful to all of them.